KU-776-596

Contents

INTRODUCTION

The *Formulary of Wound Management Products* should be used as a guide to the range of products available, their manufacturers and/or distributors, their characteristics and use in wound care.

KEY:			
	3M	=	3M Health Care Ltd
	J & J	=	Johnson and Johnson
	S & N	=	Smith and Nephew
	TM	=	Trademark in the UK
	DT	=	Drug Tariff
	POM	=	Prescription Only Medicine
	P	=	Pharmacy Only
	BNF	=	British National Formulary

If the product or a form of the product is available in the Drug Tariff, the symbols (DT) appear after the manufacturer/distributor in the title. For further information see Drug Tariff.

Addresses and telephone numbers of manufacturers/distributors can be found before the index in the BNF. Appendix 8, Wound Management Products and Elastic Hosiery, in the BNF (September 2000) contains additional information.

The *Formulary of Wound Management Products* will be regularly updated on the Euromed website as new products are launched and further technical information becomes available: www.euromed.uk.com/formulary.htm

The information in this booklet is issued on the understanding that it is the best available on the date of compilation. Whilst every effort has been made to ensure the accuracy of the text, no responsibility can be accepted for inaccuracies, omissions or errors. The opinions expressed are entirely those of the author.

The author is Director of Pharmaceutical Public Health, North Wales Health Authority, Preswylfa, Hendy Road, Mold, Flintshire CH7 1PZ.

FORMULARY OF WOUND MANAGEMENT PRODUCTS

ABSORBENT DRESSINGS
conventional dry dressings e.g.
- **Absorbent Cotton BP:** hospital quality absorbent cotton balls and rolls; should not be used for wound cleansing
- **Gamgee:** pad of cotton wool enclosed in cotton gauze; soft and absorbent; allows strike through
- **Gauze:** open-weave cotton swabs and ribbon; gauze packing is uncomfortable to apply and to remove; capillary loops may grow into fabric of the dressing; when in place it can dry out and harden
- **Gauze and Cellulose Wadding:** multi-layered cellulose wadding enclosed in absorbent cotton gauze
- **Lint:** cotton cloth with a raised nap on one side and an unlinted wound surface side; not recommended for wound management
- use only on clean dry wounds or as secondary dressings to provide padding or protection over low-adherent dressings
- should not be used directly on the surface of a moist wound
- specifically designed to remove exudate and debris from the wound – highly absorbent
- need to be changed frequently (every 12 hours) and skilled nursing care is required
- fail to meet many of the criteria of an "ideal dressing" i.e. they allow strike through, they shed fibres into the wound, they adhere to the wound base and they dehydrate the wound (*see* appendix)

ACETIC ACID
see ANTISEPTICS
- 2–5% solution applied twice daily as a wet-to-dry dressing
- can cause quite severe stinging
- specifically effective against *Pseudomonas aeruginosa* but little effect on other organisms whose numbers may increase[1,2]
- effectiveness is short-lived
- the activity of this relatively weak acid may be the result of changing the pH of the wound environment, thus inhibiting the organism's growth, rather than a direct bactericidal effect

ACTICO (COHESIVE) (Activa Health Care, DT)
- short stretch compression bandage

ACTISORB SILVER 220 (J & J, DT)
see DEODORISING DRESSINGS (formerly called Actisorb Plus)
- 100% pure activated charcoal cloth impregnated with 220mg silver enclosed within a porous nylon sleeve ("charcoal tea bag")
- used for wounds where bacterial contamination, infection or odour is present, e.g. fungating carcinomas
- the dressing adsorbs bacteria, eliminates offensive odour and reduces excessive exudate. Silver particles control bacteria adsorbed by the charcoal cloth
- apply directly to wound surface. If the wound is producing low amounts of exudate, apply a low-adherent dressing first, then Actisorb Silver 220 and an absorbent dressing (which can be replaced whenever necessary)
- can be left *in situ* for 3–7 days, depending on the level of exudate
- should not be cut in order to shape it to the wound site (the dressing is sealed along all four edges)
- contra-indicated in patients sensitive to nylon

ACTIVHEAL (Advanced Medical Solutions)
- A range of first-aid dressings available for sale in community pharmacies:
  - Film dressings – for minor cuts, grazes and burns;
  - Hydrocolloid dressings – for minor cuts and grazes which are weeping or bleeding;
  - Alginate film dressings – to aid the control of bleeding from wounds;
  - Skin closures and films – for deeper cuts;
  - Blister dressing with Tea Tree Oil – to prevent or treat blisters;
  - Family first-aid kits – contain a selection of the above dressings;
  - Burn dressings

ADHESIVES (TISSUE)
see DERMABOND, INDERMIL
- contain cyanoacrylate compounds including bucrylate, enbucrilate and mecrylate
- polymerise in an exothermic reaction on contact with a fluid or basic substance, forming a strong, flexible, waterproof bond; in rare cases, the heat may burn
- indicated for simple lacerations that otherwise might require the use of fine sutures, staples or skin strips

- produces similar cosmetic results to suturing
- a needleless and painless method of wound repair which does not require follow up visits for suture removal
- provides the strength of approximated, healed tissue at 7 days, in just minutes
- special care is required to ensure that the wound edges are well apposed so that no adhesive gets between the wound edges; after application, wound edges are held together for at least 30 seconds
- in the event of accidental adhesion of the skin or lips the bonded surfaces should be immersed in warm soapy water, the surfaces peeled or rolled apart with the aid of a spatula, and the adhesive removed from the skin with soap and water
- there have been no reports of toxicity or carcinogenicity when used topically
- do not use on hands or over joints as repetitive movement or washing will cause the adhesive to peel off

AEROSOL SPRAYS
see BETADINE, OPSITE, SPRILON
- these have become popular in the last 25 years because of cheap, disposable aerosol cans
- it is difficult to control the uniformity of spray
- they are unsafe to use on the face – there is a risk of eye damage
- multiple-antibiotic sprays containing agents such as neomycin, polymyxin or bacitracin have no place in the treatment of large wounds

ALBUFILM (S & N, DT)
- a permeable non-woven synthetic adhesive tape

ALBUPORE (S & N, DT)
- a permeable, non-woven, hypoallergenic, surgical adhesive tape

ALCOHOL
- fixes skin cells and delays wound healing
- the use of alcohol-based preparations should be restricted to prophylactic skin disinfection before needle insertions or surgical procedures[3]

ALGINATE DRESSINGS
see ALGISITE M, ALGOSTERIL, ARGLAES ISLAND DRESSING, COMFEEL PLUS, CURASORB, KALTOGEL, KALTOSTAT, MELGISORB, NU-GEL, PURILON, SEASORB, SORBALGON, SORBSAN, SUPRASORB A, TEGAGEN[4, 5, 6]

- manufactured from various varieties of seaweeds which contain large quantities of alginates. Seaweeds have been used for many generations by sailors as dressings for wounds
- alginic acid consists of a polymer containing mannuronic and guluronic acid residues. Alginates rich in mannuronic acid (like Sorbsan, Algisite M) form soft flexible gels which can be rinsed away whereas those which are rich in guluronic acid (like Kaltostat) form firmer gels making removal in one piece, easy
- some dressings contain:
  - calcium alginate e.g. Algisite M, Algosteril, Arglaes Island, Curasorb, Sorbalgon, Sorbsan, Suprasorb, Tegagen,
  - calcium-sodium alginate e.g. Kaltostat, Kaltogel, Melgisorb and Seasorb
  - alginate-hydrocolloid combinations e.g. Comfeel Plus
  - alginate-hydrogel combinations e.g. Nu-Gel, Purilon
- when in contact with wound secretions containing sodium ions, the insoluble calcium alginate is partially converted to soluble sodium alginate through the process of ion exchange (calcium/sodium) into a hydrophilic gel
- highly absorbent – most appropriate for medium to heavily exuding wounds. Only used on exuding wounds as alginates are not suitable for wounds which are very dry or covered with hard necrotic tissue
- can be used on infected wounds
- some have haemostatic properties, e.g. Algosteril, Kaltostat – bleeding can be reduced by contact with an alginate for 10 minutes, removal and replacement with another alginate dressing
- do not tightly pack the wound as the gel will conform to the shape of the wound
- this gel provides an ideal moist environment and allows pain-free dressing changes; the gel ensures that dressing changes do not disturb fresh granulation tissue
- some patients experience a mild "burning" sensation when the dressing is first applied. This may be prevented by moistening the dressing (after application) with sodium chloride 0.9% solution
- recommended that the dressing be changed daily at first then once every 2–3 days or twice weekly as healing proceeds; infected wounds should be changed at least once daily
- most require a secondary dressing
- absorbency and tensile strength of six alginates were assessed in a laboratory comparison. Sorbsan most readily dispersed in saline while Tegagel showed very little tendency to disperse. Kaltostat was intermediate between Sorbsan and Tegagel. Tegagel and Kaltostat are more likely to be removed from the

wound in one piece than Sorbsan. The results indicate very different properties which may help in the selection of the appropriate product for a particular wound[7]

- four alginates showed significant differences in important handling characteristics and did not differ significantly in their effect on epithelialisation using a standardised partial-thickness wound model in the domestic pig. More wound fluid was spread laterally with Sorbsan. Algosteril adhered more than Comfeel Alginate. Kaltostat left more dressing residues on the wound surface at dressing removal than Comfeel Alginate[8]
- histological analysis has demonstrated that prolonged tissue oedema is characterised by the incorporation of alginate (Kaltostat) fibres surrounded by a giant cell foreign body reaction; these fibres seem to disappear as the wound matures[9]

ALGISITE M (S & N, DT)
see ALGINATES

- calcium alginate, non-woven dressing and rope containing fast-gelling, high mannuronic acid fibres
- made by a needling process which produces a soft, conformable dressing with less fibre shed and high integrity when wet
- used on full and partial thickness wounds with medium to heavy exudate
- absorbs 13 times its own weight in exudate
- can stay in place for up to seven days

ALGOSTERIL (Beiersdorf, DT)
see ALGINATES

- a sterile, non-woven, calcium alginate dressing
- designed to treat heavily exuding, infected wounds
- ideal for bleeding wounds
- showed better healing rates than dextranomer paste in a prospective, randomised, controlled trial of 92 patients with full-thickness pressure ulcers[10]
- manufactured in 4 sizes (2 of which are in the DT)
- **Algosteril Rope:** 30cm/2g available in the DT

ALLDRESS (Mölnlycke)
see NON/LOW ADHERENT DRESSINGS

- a protective, absorbent dressing with an adhesive border and a non-woven middle layer
- highly absorbent wound pad

- intended for use as a secondary dressing (although it can be used as a general dressing for medium to high exudate)
- polyurethane backing film which is showerproof
- available in 3 sizes: 10x10cm, 15x15cm and 15x20cm

ALLEVYN ADHESIVE (S & N, DT)
see ALLEVYN and FOAM DRESSINGS
- sterile, polyurethane foam, film dressing with an adhesive border and a low allergy adhesive
- indicated for light to medium exuding wounds
- also available as an anatomically shaped sacral dressing
- in a randomised comparison comparing Allevyn Adhesive with Granuflex, data indicate that both dressings are easy and convenient to apply; absorbency and ease of removal were better with Allevyn; wear times were similar[11]

ALLEVYN CAVITY WOUND DRESSING (S & N, DT)
see ALLEVYN and FOAM DRESSINGS
- made from a matrix of highly absorbent, polyurethane foam "chips" separated from the wound by low-adherent, perforated film
- designed to overcome the problems associated with dressing deep wounds, e.g. pressure ulcers, leg ulcers, surgical incisions and excisions, pilonidal sinuses
- highly absorbent and is designed to manage medium to heavily exuding wounds
- conforms easily to fill cavity
- requires a secondary dressing, e.g. tape, film etc.
- can remain in place for up to 7 days – dressings should not be re-used
- available in DT in circular and tubular shapes
- Allevyn Cavity Wound dressing and Silastic Foam have been compared[12]

ALLEVYN HYDROCELLULAR (S & N, DT)
see ALLEVYN, FOAM DRESSINGS
- a hydrophilic, polyurethane dressing with a trilaminate structure:-
  - a three-dimensional, polyurethane, low-adherent wound interface
  - a central hydrophilic, foam, absorbent layer; the foam absorbs and retains exudate not only by capillary action but also by absorption of fluid into the molecular structure of the foam
  - an outer polyurethane film consisting of two thin layers of Opsite film
- mainly used on low – medium exuding granulating wounds, e.g. venous leg ulcers
- can be cut to shape for use on awkward areas, e.g. heels

- white, patterned face is applied to the wound (pink surface outwards)
- capable of absorbing and retaining large volumes of fluid (several times its own weight) even under a compression bandage
- fluid will not strike through the outer layer but water vapour is lost
- can normally be left in place for about seven days (depending on the volume of exudate)
- indicates when it requires changing, without the need for removal
- in pilonidal sinus excision wounds, both Allevyn and Kaltostat were found to be easy to use, effective and acceptable to patients and clinicians[13]
- **Allevyn Heel and Allevyn Sacral:** also available

ALLEVYN LM (S & N, DT)
see ALLEVYN, FOAM DRESSINGS
- a polyurethane foam film dressing with a non-adhesive wound contact layer
- used for granulating wounds with low to medium exudate
- can stay in place for up to 5 days
- can be used in conjunction with compression therapy
- square and rectangular, non-adhesive dressings available

ALLEVYN TRACHEOSTOMY (S & N)
see ALLEVYN and FOAM DRESSINGS
- pre-cut dressing for tracheostomy tubes and wound drains

AMNION
see SKIN SUBSTITUTES
- human extra-embryonic fetal membranes composed of:-
  - an inner, amniotic membrane – the amnion, and
  - an outer membrane – the chorion
- amnion is a true biological dressing which is available cheaply if an obstetric unit is on site
- its preparation is time-consuming, tedious and labour-intensive
- adheres to the wound so it is difficult to remove
- not recommended because of the danger of HIV infection

ANABACT (Cambridge Health Care, POM)
see ANTIBACTERIALS, METROTOP, METRONIDAZOLE, NEUTRATOP
- metronidazole gel 0.75% containing hydroxybenzoates (parabens) and propylene glycol

- use now extended for the treatment of gravitational and decubitus ulcers as well as the deodorisation of fungating, malodorous tumours
- apply to wound twice daily
- can be re-used for single patient use up to 28 days

ANAFLEX (Geistlich Pharma, P)
see ANTISEPTICS

- water-miscible cream containing 10% w/w polynoxylin
- polynoxylin is a condensation product of formaldehyde and urea and may act by the release of formaldehyde
- broad spectrum antimicrobial agent active against Gram-negative and Gram-positive bacteria as well as against fungi
- used to treat minor infected cuts and abrasions
- a burning sensation has been reported when applied to broken skin
- applied once or twice a day

ANTIBACTERIALS
see ANABACT, FLAMAZINE, METRONIDAZOLE, METROTOP, NEUTRATOP

ANTIBIOTICS
see BACTROBAN, CICATRIN, FUCIDIN, FUCIDIN INTERTULLE, GRANEODIN, SOFRA-TULLE

- characteristics of the ideal topical antibiotic:[15]
  - broad spectrum of activity
  - novel mode of action
  - low incidence of bacterial resistance
  - lack of cross-resistance with other antibiotics
  - low incidence of skin sensitisation
  - lack of skin irritation and toxicity
  - acts in the presence of serous discharge
  - not available in a systemic formulation
  - not chemically related to other antibiotics available in systemic form
  - cost effective
- as a general rule, antibiotics should not be applied topically, but given systemically
- there are two main hazards associated with their use – resistance and sensitivity reactions
- controlled use of topical antibiotics will eliminate some of the problems caused by plasmid transfer and induction of antibiotic resistance by

inappropriate use; this will reduce sensitivity reactions which can cause considerable harm and delay healing
- multiple-antibiotic sprays containing agents such as neomycin, polymyxin or bacitracin have no place in the treatment of large wounds. Neomycin can be absorbed in sufficient quantities to produce serious toxic effects
- antibiotics are less toxic to cultured human fibroblasts than antiseptics[14]

ANTISEPTICS
see ACETIC ACID, ANAFLEX, BETADINE, CETRIMIDE, CHLORHEXIDINE, INADINE, MEDI-PREP, MERCUROCHROME, PHENOXYETHANOL, POVIDERM, POVIDONE-IODINE, PROFLAVINE, SILVER NITRATE, STERIPOD CHLORHEXIDINE/CETRIMIDE, SUDOCREM, UNISEPT, VIDENE
- the ideal antiseptic[16]:
  - kills a wide range of micro-organisms
  - is effective over a wide range of dilutions
  - is non-toxic to human tissues
  - does not easily cause local or systemic sensitivity reactions
  - acts rapidly
  - works efficiently, even in the presence of organic material (pus, blood, soap)
  - is inexpensive
  - has a long shelf life
- traditional antiseptics may have toxic effects on tissues and may delay the healing process[14,17]
- antiseptics are more toxic to cultured human fibroblasts than antibiotics[14]
- avoid alcoholic solutions
- for topical use, antiseptics used judiciously and sparingly are preferable to antibiotics but irrigation of wounds with antiseptics has very little effect[18, 19]
- some antiseptics may be used for short periods only on a rotational basis to avoid the establishment of any particular micro-organism
- chlorhexidine and povidone-iodine are topical antiseptics of choice[18]
- a randomised controlled trial has shown that skin preparation with alcoholic chlorhexidine is more efficacious that skin preparation with aqueous povidone-iodine in reducing contamination of blood cultures[20]

APLIGRAF (Novartis Pharma AG, USA)
see SKIN SUBSTITUTES
- a bovine collagen fibroblast – containing matrix integrated with a sheet of stratified human epithelium

- also available as Graftskin or Testskin (Organogenesis Inc., Canton, Massachusetts)
- the fibroblasts in the "dermis" and keratinocytes in the "epidermis" are viable, reproducing cells originating from screened neonatal foreskin
- total manufacturing time is about 17–20 days
- morphologically, biochemically and metabolically similar to human skin
- when used as a skin substitute for the *in vitro* testing of commercial products, Apligraf demonstrated properties similar to those of human skin
- clinical experience is available in treating wounds caused by the surgical removal of skin cancers or keratoacanthomas and in the treatment of venous ulcers
- in the USA, an FDA panel has recommended unconditional approval for the treatment of venous leg ulcers

AQUACEL (ConvaTec, DT)
see HYDROCOLLOIDS

- a soft, sterile, non-woven pad or ribbon dressing composed entirely of hydrocolloid fibres (sodium carboxymethylcellulose)
- indicated as a primary dressing for the management of medium to highly exuding wounds. May also be used on clinically infected wounds
- applied directly to the wound overlapping the surrounding skin by at least 1cm
- should be changed when it becomes saturated with exudate or by 7 days
- very absorbent – 50% higher than alginates. Converts to a soft coherent gel sheet which retains its integrity during handling
- requires a secondary dressing
- in a randomised trial comparing Aquacel with Kaltostat, the data suggest that Aquacel may have a significantly longer wear time and reduced frequency of dressing change in patients with exuding leg ulcers[21]

AQUAFORM (Maersk, DT)
see HYDROGELS

- an amorphous, starch-based hydrogel consisting of 3.5% starch-grafted polymer in an aqueous base with 20% propylene glycol as an humectant and preservative
- suitable for use at all stages of wound healing from debridement of necrotic tissue to formation of granulation tissue
- should be changed at least every one to three days
- gel tends to dry and disintegrate
- the fluid handling properties of Aquaform and Intrasite Gel have been compared in an *in vitro* study[22]
- sterile, clear premixed gel available in single use 15g tubes (DT)

ARGLAES (Maersk)
see VAPOUR-PERMEABLE FILMS
- a controlled release film dressing containing 10% w/w polymer silver ions which are released at a constant rate until the film is removed from the wound site (5–7 days); this exerts a constant antibacterial effect
- darker in colour than standard film dressings due to natural tinting of the film by the silver ingredient
- used for the management of medium to heavily exuding wounds
- **Arglaes Island Dressing:** a combined Arglaes film dressing with a calcium alginate pad
- **Arglaes Powder:** 15g

ASERBINE (Goldshield)
- a mixture of malic, benzoic and salicylic acids in propylene glycol
- available as a solution and a cream; the solution is approximately six times stronger than the cream
- the cream is applied after cleansing with the solution – usually twice daily
- used to deslough and cleanse wounds; has antibacterial properties
- causes cleavage between dead and living tissue probably due to its low pH (2.4)
- may irritate skin around the ulcer e.g. urticarial rash
- during extensive use, wound and skin may become macerated

ASKINA BIOFILM TRANSPARENT (B Braun, DT)
see HYDROCOLLOIDS
- thin semi-permeable transparent hydrocolloid dressing containing carboxymethylcellulose, polyisobutylene and a polyurethane backing
- used for light to medium exuding wounds
- may be left in place for up to 6–8 days (in the absence of exudate) before changing
- available as square and rectangular dressings

ASKINA DERM (B Braun, DT)
see VAPOUR-PERMEABLE FILMS

ASKINA JET SALINE (B Braun, DT)
see SODIUM CHLORIDE
- 0.9% sterile sodium chloride (saline) irrigation and cleansing fluid

ASKINA SPRAY BUFFERED (B Braun, DT)
see SODIUM CHLORIDE
- sodium chloride (saline) aerosol for irrigation

ASKINA TRANSORBENT (B Braun, DT)
see FOAMS
- adhesive polyurethane foam film dressing
- used for light to medium exuding wounds
- may be left in place for up to 7 days before changing
- available as square and rectangular dressings (with or without borders) and as a sacral dressing

ASPIRIN
- in a double-blind randomised trial in 20 patients, enteric-coated aspirin 300mg daily, with standardised compression bandaging, improved the healing rate of chronic venous ulcers[23]
- however, the validity of the findings has been challenged[24, 25]

ATRAUMAN (Hartmann)
see TULLE (NON-MEDICATED) DRESSINGS
- a non-medicated polyester sterile tulle dressing
- impregnated with an ointment containing caprylic, capric, stearic triglycerides; caprylic, capric, isostearic, adipic triglycerides (does not contain vaseline or paraffins)
- used for superficial wounds e.g. cuts, lacerations, abrasions
- available in 3 sizes: 5x5cm, 7.5x10cm and 10x20cm

BACTIGRAS (S & N, DT)
see CHLORHEXIDINE, SEROTULLE
- sterilised Chlorhexidine Gauze Dressing BP impregnated with white soft paraffin containing 0.5% w/w chlorhexidine acetate
- active against a wide range of Gram-positive/negative organisms
- effective *in vitro* and *in vivo* against MRSA
- acquired resistance has been reported
- can be used on large wounds up to 10% body area
- the dressing tends to adhere
- poor release of the chlorhexidine from the hydrophobic paraffin base has been reported when tested by an *in vitro* zone diffusion technique[26]

BACTROBAN (SmithKline Beecham, POM)
see ANTIBIOTICS
- two different products are available with different uses:
  - sterile 2% mupirocin ointment (polyethylene glycol base) for primary bacterial skin infections (impetigo)

- sterile 2% cream for secondary infected traumatic lesions
- not related to any other antibiotic in use
- active against those organisms responsible for the majority of skin infections, e.g. *Staphylococcus aureus*, including methicillin-resistant strains (MRSA), other staphylococci and streptococci. It is also active against Gram-negative organisms such as *Escherichia coli* and *Haemophilus influenzae*
- there have been reports of spreading resistance to mupirocin among *Staph. aureus*
- applied up to 3 times daily for short courses only (up to 10 days)
- mupirocin (pseudomonic acid) is available exclusively as a topical antibiotic
- side effects are limited to local reactions (in less than 3% of patients) and results indicate that the polyethylene glycol base is the probable causative factor
- sensitisation to mupirocin has so far not been reported
- may be some stinging, burning or itching on application
- used for bacterial skin infections, e.g. impetigo, folliculitis, furunculosis. Its precise place in wound management remains to be established. Limited evidence suggests that mupirocin may be as effective as the current topical antibacterials used but more controlled, comparative studies are needed. Bactroban is probably useful for topical treatment of secondary infected traumatic lesions such as small lacerations, sutured wounds or abrasions (up to 10cm in length or 100cm square in area), caused by susceptible strains of *Staph. aureus* and *Streptococcus pyogenes*

BANDAGES (FOUR-LAYER)
- a suitable option for patients with venous ulcers but all patients require a thorough assessment
- the four-layer system can be left in place for up to a week
- inexperienced practitioners are more likely to apply dangerously high levels of pressure with single-layer bandages than with a Charing Cross or Profore multilayer system[27]
- community-based leg ulcer clinics with trained nurses using four-layer bandaging are more effective than traditional home-based treatment[28]
- compression treatment increases the healing of ulcers compared with no compression. Multi-layered systems are more effective than single-layered systems. High compression is more effective than low compression. No clear differences in the effectiveness of different types of compression systems (multilayer and short stretch bandages and Unna's boot) have been shown[29]
- *Effective Health Care Bulletin* summarises the results of research on the

effectiveness and cost-effectiveness of different forms of compression in the treatment of venous ulceration; on interventions to prevent recurrence; and on methods of diagnosing venous ulceration[30]

- in an evaluation of cost-effectiveness of using Profore and Charing Cross systems compared with 'usual care', both four-layer systems were more cost-effective and achieved better healing rates than usual care. Substantial potential savings were identified if four-layer bandaging was used[31]

- a number of products are now available in the Drug Tariff and can be used as components in a multi-layer bandaging system. Multi-layer bandaging "kits" are not prescribable as such. However, if prescribers wish to prescribe the individual components they are free to do so; and pharmacists are free to meet a prescription with a "kit" if the content of the kit exactly matches the components prescribed.

- typically, components of a multi-layer bandaging system are applied over a wound contact layer and are:
  - First layer: natural orthopaedic wool layer which is used to absorb exudate and redistribute pressure around the ankle. Applied in a loose spiral;
  - Second layer: a crepe bandage which increases absorbency and smooths the orthopaedic wool layer. Applied in a spiral;
  - Third layer: a light compression bandage;
  - Fourth layer: an elastic, cohesive bandage which maintains the four layers in place

- **Charing Cross multi-layer system:**[32]
  1. Orthopaedic wool such as Velband (J & J) or Soffban (S & N)
  2. Crepe (10cm)
  3. Elset (Seton, 10cm) – elastic, conformable compression bandage applied at mid-stretch in a figure of eight from toe to knee with a 50% overlap
  4. Coban (3M, 10cm) – lightweight, elastic, cohesive bandage applied at mid-stretch with a 50% overlap

- **Hospi-Four (Millpledge Healthcare, DT)**
  1. Ortho-Band Plus – sub-compression wadding bandage
  2. Hospicrepe – cotton stretch bandage
  3. Litetex + – type 3a compression bandage
  4. AAA–Flex – lightweight, elastic, cohesive bandage

- **K-Four (Parema, DT)**
  1. K-Soft – sub-compression wadding bandage
  2. K-Lite – light support bandage (type 2)
  3. K-Plus – a type 3A light compression bandage
  4. Ko-Flex – cohesive flexible bandage

- **Profore system (S & N, DT). For ankle circumference 18–25cm:-**
  1. Soffban – natural orthopaedic wool layer
  2. Soffcrepe – crepe bandage
  3. Litepress – a type 3A light compression bandage
  4. Co-Plus – cohesive flexible bandage
  Note: there are also other Profore systems for ankle circumferences less than 18cm, 25–30cm and greater than 30cm; also for reduced compression for mixed aetiology ulcers – **Profore Lite**
- **System 4 (SSL, DT):** For ankle circumference 18–25cm:
  1. Softexe, wadding bandage
  2. Setocrepe (10cm)
  3. Elset (10cm) – elastic, conformable compression bandage applied at mid-stretch in a figure of eight from toe to knee with a 50% overlap.
  4. Coban (3M, 10cm) – type 3b, lightweight, elastic, cohesive bandage applied at mid-stretch with a 50% overlap
  Note: there are also other System 4 combinations for ankle circumferences less than 18cm, 25–30cm and greater than 30cm
- **Ultra Four (Robinson Healthcare, DT).** For ankle circumference 18–25cm:-
  1. Sohfast, soft absorbent bandage – applied in a spiral format from toe to knee with a 50% overlap and no pressure
  2. K-Lite, crepe bandage – applied in a spiral format from toe to knee with a 50% overlap
  3. K-Plus, long stretch bandage – applied in a figure of eight format from toe to knee with a 50% overlap at mid stretch
  4. Cohfast non latex cohesive bandage – applied in a spiral format from toe to knee with a 50% overlap at mid stretch

BANDAGES (EXTENSIBLE)

- a range of bandages which have extensible properties varying from very low strength for retention of primary wound contact materials, through to strong compression bandages. The classes (types 3a, 3b, 3c, 3d) are designed to give the pressures specified and 3a – 3c match those of the compression hosiery specifications of the Drug Tariff.

- **TYPE 1** (conforming stretch bandages): have a simple dressing retention function, conforming well to limbs and joints without restricting movement or applying significant pressure.
  Examples: Crinx, Easifix, K-Band, Kling, Slinky, Stayform, Texband

- **TYPE 2** (light support bandages, sometimes called short- or minimal-stretch bandages): used to prevent the formation of oedema and give support in the management of sprains and strains. They are not suitable for applying compression or reducing oedema.
  Examples: Crepe BP, Elastocrepe, Flexocrepe, Grip, Leukocrepe

- **TYPE 3a** (light compression bandage): Equivalent to Class 1 Compression Hosiery. Compression at ankle 14–17 mmHg. Indications are for superficial or early varices and varicoses during pregnancy
  Examples: Elset, K-Plus, Litetex +

- **TYPE 3b** (moderate compression bandages): Equivalent to Class 2 Compression Hosiery. Compression at ankle 18–24 mmHg. Indications are for varices of medium severity, ulcer treatment and prevention, mild oedema and varicoses during pregnancy.
  Examples: Molastic Light, Venopress

- **TYPE 3c** (high compression bandage): Equivalent to Class 3 Compression Hosiery. Compression at ankle 25–35 mmHg. Indications are for gross varices, post thrombotic venous insufficiency, gross oedema and ulcer treatment and prevention.
  Examples: Bilastic Medium, Setopress, Surepress, Tensopress

- **TYPE 3d** (extra high compression bandage): Compression at ankle 35–60 mm Hg. Indicated for severe lymphoedema.
  Examples: Bilastic Forte, Blue Line Varico, Elastoweb, Molastic Forte

BARRIER FILMS (skin protectants/sealants)
see CAVILLON, CLINISHIELD, COMFEEL SKIN CARE, OPSITE SPRAY, SKIN-PREP, SPRILON, SUPERSKIN

- protective polymers dissolved in a fast-drying carrier solvent which ideally should:
  - be non-cytotoxic
  - be pain-free on application to broken
  - protect skin from moisture, urine etc.
  - protect from skin stripping e.g. adhesive tape trauma
  - be compatible with clothing
- following application, the solvent quickly evaporates, leaving the polymer on the skin
- all of the newer barriers are considerably more expensive than the traditional

barriers such as Conotrane, Sudocrem, Drapolene, Metanium (it is doubtful if these are more effective than the traditional zinc ointments)

BETADINE (SSL, P)
see ANTISEPTICS and POVIDONE-IODINE
- wide range of preparations containing povidone-iodine including:-
  - antiseptic solution (10%) – aqueous solution
  - alcoholic solution (10%)
  - paint (10%) – alcoholic solution
  - ointment (10%) – water miscible base
  - cream (5%)
  - dry powder spray (2.5%)

BIATAIN (Coloplast, DT)
see FOAMS
- polyurethane foam film dressing with or without an adhesive border
- similar profile to other foam dressings
- the adhesive dressing has a skin-friendly hydrocolloid adhesive and a central absorbent pad with a waterproof semipermeable film backing
- the non-adhesive dressing can be used on fragile skin
- used for light to medium exuding wounds
- can be used under compression bandages
- may be left in place for up to 7 days

BIOBRANE (CliniMed)
see SKIN SUBSTITUTES
- a biocomposite of an ultra thin, semipermeable silicone membrane mechanically bonded to a flexible knitted nylon fabric. A non-toxic mixture of highly purified peptides derived from porcine dermal collagen is bonded to the elastic membrane
- membrane is highly flexible and conformable with excellent adherent properties and a hydrophilic, biocompatible surface; membrane is vapour-permeable
- membrane is applied FABRIC (DULL) SIDE DOWN, wrinkle free against the wound surface with slight tension (using staples or tape to immobilise it). Biobrane is designed to adhere to a properly prepared wound bed and to remain in place throughout the course of re-epithelialisation without changing the dressing
- available in 4 different sizes
- **Biobrane Gloves:** available in four different sizes

- **Biobrane-L:** available in three different sizes for wounds where less adhesion is desired e.g. meshed autografts

BIOCLUSIVE (J & J, DT)
see VAPOUR-PERMEABLE FILMS
- consists of a thin polyurethane membrane coated with acrylic adhesive
- can be eased apart if it clings to itself during application

BIPP (distributed by Oxford Pharmaceuticals)
- Bismuth Subnitrate and Iodoform Paste BPC 1954
- a smooth, yellow, non-sterile paste containing Bismuth Subnitrate BPC (1 part), Iodoform USNF (2 parts) and liquid paraffin (1 part by weight)
- iodoform exerts a mild disinfectant action and bismuth subnitrate has an astringent action but there is no agreement about its mode of action
- used as a mild disinfectant primarily for packing cavities in ENT surgery
- contra-indicated where there is hypersensitivity to iodoform, iodine or bismuth
- bismuth encephalopathy has been reported; some reports have ascribed the neurological effects to the iodoform component
- available as a paste (30g tubes) and sterile, X-ray detectable gauze (2 sizes)

BLISTER TREATMENT (SSL)
- non-medicated hydrocolloid absorbent dressing for the treatment and prevention of blisters
- available in small and medium sizes

BURNZAP (Derma Technology)
- a mousse comprising a mixture of paraffin oils and waxes in a spray can
- first-aid treatment for burn injuries which provides local cooling for at least 10 minutes[33, 34]

CALCIUM GLUCONATE GEL
- a formulation containing 2.5% w/w calcium gluconate and 3% w/w hydroxyethylcellulose as a gel-forming agent with no preservatives was found to be the most appropriate gel for topical treatment of hydrofluoric acid burns[35]

CARBOFLEX (ConvaTec, DT)
see DEODORISING DRESSINGS
- a sterile non-adhesive dressing consisting of 5 layers:

- ethylene methyl acrylate film
- absorbent padding
- activated charcoal cloth
- ethylene methyl acrylate film (which delays strike through)
- absorbent wound contact layer containing Kaltostat and Aquacel
- used for the management of malodorous acute and chronic wounds
- may be used as a primary dressing for shallow wounds or with deeper wounds as a secondary dressing over wound fillers
- may be used on infected malodorous wounds under medical supervision together with appropriate antibiotic therapy and frequent monitoring of the wound
- should not be cut to size
- place the fibrous (non-shiny) surface on wound
- with non-infected wounds, may be left undisturbed for up to three days
- available in three sizes: 10 x 10cm, 8 x 15cm (oval) and 15 x 20cm

CARBONET (S & N)
see DEODORISING DRESSINGS
- multi-layered, low adherent, absorbent, deodorising dressing:
  - low-adherent interface of Tricotex
  - absorbent layer of Melolin fleece
  - layer of activated charcoal cloth
- for discharging infected and malodorous wounds
- is highly conformable and can be cut to size
- apply knitted side of dressing to wound

CARBOPAD V C (Vernon-Carus, DT)
see DEODORISING DRESSINGS
- consists of a sterile dressing of:
  - low-adherent layer
  - an active layer of 100% activated charcoal cloth
  - a vapour-permeable film
  - a white cover to distinguish the outer side of the dressing from that facing the wound
- combines the advantages of a film dressing and an activated charcoal dressing
- used for the treatment of infected, discharging and malodorous wounds; the dark, smooth side of the dressing is placed on the wound
- initially change dressing frequently (1 – 3 times a day); after 2 – 3 weeks dressing changes can be made less frequently
- available in two sizes which should not be cut to size

22

CAVI-CARE (S & N, DT)
see FOAMS
- a conformable foam cavity dressing (formerly known as Silastic Foam)[36]
- a dual sachet dressing consisting of polymers (polydimethylsiloxanes), platinum catalyst, inhibitor and ethanol (10g sachet); polymers, cross-linkers (copolysiloxanes), inhibitor and ethanol (10g sachet)
- the clear fluid contents of the sachets are mixed vigorously for 5–15 seconds. The mixture turns opaque, foams and increases in volume and should be poured into the wound within 30 seconds of mixing. The dressing will set within 3–5 minutes and should not be touched or removed during this period
- skill is needed to mix and mould the stent or bung. The final volume of the stent is approximately four times the volume of the original mixture
- normally used in open deep wounds or cavities of regular shape without underlying tracts or sinuses[36]. It should not be used in dry wounds, mucous membranes, fistulae or sinuses from which the bung cannot be removed; this may lead to a foreign body reaction
- it has the physical and protective functions of gauze packing and is an excellent alternative to packing wounds with ribbon gauze (dressing conforms to shape of wound or cavity)
- a new stent needs to be made approximately every week to allow for wound contraction
- depending on discharge, the stent must be removed from wound at least every 48 hours for rinsing with clean water, soaking in 0.5% aqueous chlorhexidine solution for at least 10 minutes, and then a final rinse with water to remove the antiseptic[37]
- patient manageable; saves nursing time and repeat visits to the clinic
- avoid contact with eyes and with fabric and clothing (it is not removable)
- available in 20g units (2x10g sachets)
- Silastic foam and Allevyn Cavity wound dressing have been compared[12]

CAVILON (3M, DT)
see BARRIER FILMS
- a no-sting, protective, transparent barrier film
- indicated as a protective interface between the skin and bodily wastes, fluids and adhesive dressings and tapes
- provides pain-free protection on broken skin
- is non-cytotoxic and will not interfere with wound healing. It can provide protection for pressure sores, incontinence dermatitis, stoma sites, venous ulcers, adhesion trauma/skin stripping and for peri-wound areas

- product is dispersed in a skin-friendly, non-stinging solvent which is alcohol-free but dries rapidly
- under normal use, requires re-application only once every 48–72 hours
- does not require removal before re-application
- available as a single use foam applicator (1ml and 3ml) and as a pump spray (28ml) for larger areas

CELLONA UNDERCAST PADDING (Vernon-Carus Ltd, DT)
- a sub-compression wadding bandage used as a component of multi-layer compression bandaging

CETRIMIDE
see ANTISEPTICS, STERIPOD CHLORHEXIDINE/CETRIMIDE
- a quaternary ammonium compound
- constituent of many products, mostly in combination with chlorhexidine e.g. Hibicet Hospital Concentrate, Steripod Chlorhexidine and Cetrimide, Tisept and Travasept
- has a wide range of bactericidal activity against Gram-positive and some Gram-negative organisms
- 1% solutions are used for their emulsifying and detergent properties especially in A & E Units for dirty wounds
- cytotoxic to mouse fibroblast cells even at low concentrations[38]
- side effects: skin irritation and occasionally sensitisation; should be used with caution – not for routine cleansing of non-infected wounds

CHLORASOL (SSL)
see CHLORINATED SOLUTIONS
- sachets of sterile sodium hypochlorite solution containing 0.3% available chlorine with a pH of 11–11.5
- broad-spectrum antimicrobial agent
- stable for 18 months if stored between 5° and 25°C away from direct light
- irritant – not recommended for wound care

CHLORHEXIDINE (many manufacturers)
see ANTISEPTICS
- effective against a wide range of Gram-positive and Gram-negative organisms and some viruses and fungi but not spores. In a comparative trial against 33 strains of methicillin resistant *Staphylococcus aureus* (MRSA), chlorhexidine achieved full efficacy against only 3 strains of MRSA, whilst povidone-iodine was fully effective against every single strain on trial[39]

- 0.05% solutions recommended for wounds; antimicrobial activity may be reduced because of incompatibility, adsorption or in the presence of organic material
- many preparations available e.g. :
  - Gauze dressings – *see* Bactigras, Serotulle
  - Dusting powder – *see* CX Antiseptic Dusting powder
  - Chlorhexidine acetate or gluconate 0.05% solutions e.g. Unisept, Steripod Chlorhexidine
  - Chlorhexidine gluconate 0.02% solution e.g. Sterexidine
  - Solutions in combination with cetrimide (*see* CETRIMIDE)
  - Concentrated solutions e.g. Hibitane 5% concentrate
- acquired resistance reported with *Proteus mirabilis* and *Pseudomonas aeruginosa*
- side effects: sensitivity may occur, avoid contact with mucous membranes and meninges. A severe allergic reaction has been reported[40]
- a case of acute anaphylaxis, including a widespread erythematous rash, periorbital oedema, sinus tachycardia and mild angio-oedema has been reported after a dressing containing chlorhexidine acetate BP 0.5% was used to dress a burn on a patient's arm[41]
- suitable topical antiseptic for wound care but do not use alcoholic solutions

CHLORINATED SOLUTIONS
see CHLORASOL, DAKIN'S SOLUTION, EUSOL, MILTON[42, 43, 44]

- chlorine-releasing solutions are bactericidal to most Gram-positive/negative bacteria and to some spores and viruses. Their activity is reduced in the presence of organic material and in alkaline conditions
- all solutions cause a moderate to severe irritant response within 4–5 days
- at concentrations recommended for wound cleansing, sodium hypochlorite produces 100% killing of all cell types[14, 45]. Sodium hypochlorite (0.005%) is bactericidal and non-cytotoxic[14]
- are highly toxic to mouse connective tissue fibroblasts
- reduce basal cell viability under certain conditions
- significantly delay the production of collagen and prolong the acute inflammatory response in wounds healing by secondary intention
- may impair epithelial migration
- cause a complete cessation of blood flow
- have a short shelf life e.g. Eusol
- may bleach clothing and other materials
- some advocate the use of these solutions as desloughing agents for 3–4 days only; others prefer to avoid the possible disadvantages by using alternative

products having a better reputation (*see* appendix – Management of wounds and wound types)

- sodium hypochlorite dressing protocols for surgical wounds should be abandoned[46]

CICA-CARE (S & N, DT)
see SILICONE DRESSINGS

- a sterile, soft, self-adhesive, semi-occlusive silicone gel sheet – a cross-linked, polydimethylsiloxane gel
- for temporary use in the management of both new and existing hypertrophic scars (red, raised scars, not flat, white scars). Improves the appearance of red or raised scars
- also used as a prophylactic treatment on closed wounds to prevent hypertrophic or keloid scarring. It is not used on open wounds
- should be applied for 4 hours per day (first 2 days), then 8 hours per day (next 2 days). After this, wear time should be increased by 2 hours per day until a minimum of 12 hours per day is reached (if possible for 24 hours per day). The build up is necessary to acclimatise the skin to the gel sheet
- can be cut to fit the shape of the scar
- best results are usually achieved within 2–4 months
- sheets can be re-used for up to one month. They should be washed twice daily in a mild non-oily soap solution and rinsed in clean warm water
- possible complications are superficial maceration of the skin, rash and pruritus
- available for sale from community pharmacies (from March 1998)

CICATRIN (GlaxoWellcome)
see ANTIBIOTICS

- an amino-acid-antibiotic containing neomycin and bacitracin available as cream and dusting powder
- has broad spectrum of antibacterial activity
- may cause emergence of resistant strains
- absorption of neomycin may cause ototoxicity or nephrotoxicity
- bacitracin or neomycin may cause hypersensitivity reactions
- the incidence of allergic contact dermatitis with neomycin is common ranging from 1.7% to 19%
- not recommended for wound care

CLEARSITE (NDM UK)
see HYDROGELS

- a hydrophilic, biocompatible gel polymer covered with a polyurethane film marked with a 1cm grid (not removable)

- the gel is approximately 60% isotonic saline solution with approximately 20% propylene glycol and 20% polyurethane polymer
- indicated for treatment of chronic and acute wounds and for wound prevention and protection
- good absorptive capacity whilst maintaining integrity (leaving no residue in the wound)
- can remain in place for up to seven days, while remaining transparent

CLINISHIELD (CliniMed)
see BARRIER FILMS
- wipe on skin protection to protect vulnerable peristomal skin and to reduce skin trauma
- available on NHS prescription

CLINISORB ODOUR CONTROL DRESSING (Clinimed, DT)
see DEODORISING DRESSINGS
- activated charcoal cloth sandwiched between viscose rayon. Both surfaces are identical, consisting of viscose rayon coated with polyamide
- can be cut to size
- applied as a secondary dressing over a primary dressing and secured using surgical tape

COD LIVER OIL AND HONEY TULLE (Malam Labs)
- M and M Tulle; cotton gauze impregnated with cod liver oil, purified honey and 0.5% w/w hexachlorophane

COLLAGEN
see OPRASKIN, SUPRASORB C
- fibre-forming protein of mammalian connective tissue (skin, tendons, bones and cartilage) accounting for approximately 30% of the total body protein in mammals
- major component of the extracellular matrix forming an organised structure bridging the basal cells of the epidermis with the adjacent connective tissue matrix
- at least 10 different types of collagen have been identified
- collagen contributes to all phases of the wound healing process:
  - binds blood clotting factors XII and XIII
  - causes natural wound cleansing
  - attracts granulocytes and fibroblasts
  - reduces wound contraction and enhances deposition of orientated, organised collagen fibres

- slight risk of antigenicity, although this is usually low
- used as a haemostat, an absorbable suture material, artificial skin, bone filling material and as a wound dressing

COMBIDERM (ConvaTec, DT)
see HYDROCOLLOIDS
- incorporates the technological achievements of super absorbent technology with modern wound care
- a sterile, absorbent, occlusive wound dressing comprising:
  - a polyurethane film
  - Duoderm Extra Thin hydrocolloid adhesive border
  - a non-adherent, absorbent island padding containing superabsorbent polyacrylate granules, which expand and gel in contact with exudate. This holds exudate away from the skin to reduce maceration
  - a non-adherent wound contact layer
- used for chronic and acute, low to medium exuding wounds
- absorbs fluid and retains it within its structure
- resists bacterial penetration for up to 11 days thus reducing the risk of cross-infection
- can be left in place for up to 7 days
- **Combiderm-N:** non-adhesive dressing used for chronic and acute, low to medium exuding wounds especially in patients with fragile peri-ulcer skin or with sensitivity to adhesive

COMFEEL – PASTE/POWDER (Coloplast)
see COMFEEL PLUS, HYDROCOLLOIDS
- **Paste** consists of sodium carboxymethylcellulose (NaCMC) and guar gum in a vaseline base. The paste is used in conjunction with the sheets to fill wounds with substantial tissue loss (more than 5mm deep). Also indicated for debridement of moderate necrosis
- **Powder** is composed totally of absorbent ingredients: NaCMC, xanthan gum and guar gum. This has high absorptive capacity and is recommended where there are large amounts of secretions, e.g. high wound exudate

COMFEEL PLUS CONTOUR DRESSING (Coloplast, DT)
see COMFEEL PLUS ULCER, HYDROCOLLOIDS
- a Comfeel Plus Ulcer dressing consisting of an oval hydrocolloid core and a four-wing frame of thick hydrocolloid adhesive surrounding the core
- for use over awkward areas and should provide a longer wearing time

COMFEEL PLUS PRESSURE-RELIEVING DRESSING (Coloplast)
see COMFEEL PLUS ULCER, HYDROCOLLOIDS
- a combination of a Comfeel Dressing and a foam disc with detachable centre pieces attached with microporous tape; available in three sizes
- used for local pressure relief for existing pressure ulcers and prophylactically in risk sites where local pressure relief is required
- dressing should be changed when the foam backing is reduced to about 50% of original thickness by the effects of compression

COMFEEL PLUS TRANSPARENT DRESSING (Coloplast)
see COMFEEL PLUS ULCER, HYDROCOLLOIDS
- transparent version of Comfeel Plus
- thin layer of transparent, absorbent carboxymethylcellulose with a polyurethane upper film
- used for superficial wounds with medium to low exudate

COMFEEL PLUS ULCER DRESSING (Coloplast, DT)
see ALGINATES, HYDROCOLLOIDS
- a calcium alginate/sodium carboxymethylcellulose dressing in an elastic self-adhesive mass. Top layer is made from semi-permeable polyurethane film. A calcium alginate/hydrocolloid dressing
- used for light to heavily exuding wounds
- during use the colour of the sheet dressing changes from beige to white to transparent; the dressing should then be changed
- a grid implant on the polyurethane top film provides an easy method for measurement of the wound area
- Comfeel Ulcer and Granuflex products have been compared[47]
- **Contour Dressing** and **Sacral Dressing** also available

COMFEEL SKIN CARE (Coloplast, DT)
- comprises two products:
  - a protective film used by ostomy patients
  - a barrier cream (lanolin-free)

COMPEED HYDRO CURE (Coloplast)
see COMFEEL PLUS ULCER, HYDROCOLLOIDS
- skin protector patches of various types
- elastic, flexible and waterproof; should be warmed before use
- used to protect areas from blistering or as a first-aid dressing for cuts, grazes, blisters, corns, heel cracks and callouses

- available over the counter

COMPRESSION BANDAGES AND HOSIERY
see BANDAGES EXTENSIBLE and BANDAGES FOUR-LAYER

CONOTRANE (Yamanouchi)
see BARRIER FILMS
- medicated cream containing 22% dimeticone and 0.1% benzalkonium chloride
- not recommended as there are blander, less complex products available

COSMOPOR E (Hartmann, DT)
see NON/LOW-ADHERENT DRESSINGS (similar to Mepore, Primapore and Sterifix)
- absorbent, perforated dressing with adhesive border
- nine sizes available

CRAB COLLAGENASE
- prepared from the hepatopancreas of the king crab (*Paralithodes camtschatica*)
- a comparative study with four other enzyme preparations suggest that crab collagenase is useful in wound debridement[48]

CRYSTAL VIOLET (GENTIAN VIOLET)
see DYES
- early in 1987, the DoH advised manufacturers that this should not be used on mucous membranes or open wounds, but should be restricted to topical application on unbroken skin. This was because of reports that systemic absorption of these dyes is carcinogenic in animals

CURASORB (Kendall)
see ALGINATE DRESSINGS
- a soft, off-white, sterile, non-woven calcium alginate dressing
- suitable for low to heavily exuding wounds
- can absorb 20 times its own weight in exudate
- forms a gel that remains stable in the presence of exudate
- available as **Curasorb Dressing, Curasorb Plus Dressing** and **Curasorb Rope**

CURIOSIN (Gideon Richter)
- a 0.2% solution of zinc hyaluronate

- launched in Hungary during the second half 1996
- used for leg ulcers and pressure ulcers

CUTICERIN (Beiersdorf)
see NON/LOW ADHERENT DRESSING

CUTIFILM (Beiersdorf, DT)
see VAPOUR-PERMEABLE FILMS
- polyurethane film-coated with a hypoallergenic polyacrylate adhesive
- flexible carrier – ideal for wound mapping with ordinary ball-point
- **Cutifilm Plus:** vapour permeable dressing with integral wound pad

CUTILIN (Beiersdorf, DT)
see NON/LOW ADHERENT DRESSINGS
- the shiny contact layer is placed on the wound

CUTINOVA CAVITY (Beiersdorf, DT)
see HYDROACTIVE DRESSINGS
- capable of absorbing and retaining large volumes of water (up to 32 times its own weight); moulds to contours of wound as wound fluid is absorbed
- does not disintegrate in contact with wound exudate
- used for heavily exuding wounds
- designed to overcome the problems associated with dressing deep wounds
- requires secondary dressing
- frequency of dressing change is dependent on exudate level

CUTINOVA FOAM (Beiersdorf, DT)
see HYDROACTIVE DRESSINGS
- composed of two layers: a semi-permeable polyurethane film and polyurethane matrix containing super-absorbent molecules
- suitable for sensitive, delicate skin, due to light adhesion
- quick and high absorbency for medium exuding wounds
- cushioning effect and an ability to protect already damaged or sensitive skin

CUTINOVA HYDRO (Beiersdorf, DT)
see HYDROACTIVE DRESSINGS
- semi-permeable hydrocolloid dressing without an adhesive border
- composed of a polyurethane gel covered with a transparent polyurethane film
- high absorbency
- provides a barrier to bacteria and water

- used for medium to heavily exuding wounds
- dressing change is indicated by a whitish blister

CUTINOVA THIN (Beiersdorf)
see HYDROACTIVE DRESSINGS
- consists of two layers, a semi-permeable membrane, and a polyurethane matrix
- absorbs fluid quickly due to its capillary and absorbent properties
- very flexible and mouldable
- for use with low to medium exuding wounds
- semi-transparent allowing for easy monitoring of wound progress

CUTIPLAST (Beiersdorf)
see NON/LOW ADHERENT DRESSING
- wound island dressing consisting of non-woven polyester fabric coated with a polyacrylate adhesive
- available as individual sterile dressings and non-sterile rolls

CX POWDER (Adams, DT)
see CHLORHEXIDINE
- a fine powder containing Chlorhexidine acetate 1% w/w in Absorbable Dusting Powder BP
- for general skin disinfection and antisepsis; applied to affected area three times daily
- packaged in a sterile, 15g puffer pack

DAKIN'S SOLUTION (Surgical Chlorinated Soda Solution BPC)
see CHLORINATED SOLUTIONS
- a solution of chlorinated lime, sodium carbonate and boric acid containing 0.5% w/v available chlorine with a pH of 9.5
- first introduced for topical use in open wounds during World War 1 by Nobel Prize winner Alexis Carrel
- needs to be freshly prepared as it is only stable for 2–3 weeks
- not recommended for wound care

DEBRISAN BEADS (Pharmacia & Upjohn)
- hydrophilic, sterile spherical beads of dextranomer (dextran, a carbohydrate polymer cross-linked with epichlorohydrin)
- 1g of beads absorb up to 4g of exudate; capillary action carries debris and bacteria away from the wound surface; small molecules enter the beads themselves

- when the beads are fully saturated, the system returns to its original state unless replaced first with new material once or twice a day
- used only on sloughy, exuding wounds and should not be allowed to dry out
- rinsing away the soiled beads can be difficult and uncomfortable (dextranomer is not biodegradable)

DEBRISAN PASTE (Pharmacia & Upjohn)
- a sterile soft, white, granular paste consisting of dextranomer 6.4g, polyethylene glycol 600 and water to 10g
- renew according to the rate of exudation, usually twice daily to every two days
- advised method of application is cumbersome
- Intrasite Gel is more effective at promoting debridement than Debrisan Paste[49]
- Debrisan Paste and Intrasite Gel are both efficacious in the debridement of non-viable tissue. Intrasite Gel had a greater impact in reducing wound area; was superior in ease of application and removal, in reducing pain on application and removal; and in patient comfort during wear[50]

DENIDOR (Jeffreys, Miller)
see DEODORISING DRESSINGS
- activated carbon, deodorising dressing pad
- non-sterile – therefore, do not use as a primary dressing

DEODORISING CARBON DRESSINGS
see ACTISORB PLUS, CARBOFLEX, CARBONET, CARBOPAD V-C, CLINISORB, DENIDOR, LYOFOAM C (sugar and metronidazole products can also be used to control odour)
- used in the management of discharging, purulent and contaminated wounds complicated by bacterial infection and offensive odour, e.g. fungating carcinomas, leg ulcers, pressure ulcers, gangrenous lesions, etc.
- during their preparation the charcoal fibres become microporous and develop thin, slit-like pores. A high adsorptive performance results from the substantially increased total surface area which is created
- activated charcoal reduces the concentration of offensive odour to low levels
- some dressings adsorb bacteria. The precise method by which bacteria are attracted is not clear, although it has been suggested that there could be an electrostatic or physico-chemical affinity between the charcoal and the bacteria
- some dressings do not maintain a moist environment over the wound, e.g. Actisorb Plus, Denidor
- the odour adsorbing capability of five of the dressings has been assessed[51]

- anaerobic bacteria are commonly found in chronic wounds, particularly those that are infected. Several of the Gram-negative anaerobes are the primary causes of wound malodour and consequently their eradication is necessary for the elimination of malodour. Malodour severity may be increased as a consequence of aerobic and anaerobic micro-organisms working in synergy. Disruption of microbial interactions may thus be important in the control of wound malodour[52]

DERMABOND (Ethicon, DT)
see ADHESIVES (TISSUE), INDERMIL
- contains 2-octyl cyanoacrylate

DERMAFILM (Vygon UK)
see VAPOUR-PERMEABLE FILMS
- self-adhesive, sterile drape for surgery and wound dressings

DERMAGRAFT (Advanced Tissue Sciences in partnership with S & N)
see SKIN SUBSTITUTES
- a human dermal replacement consisting of new-born human fibroblast cells cultured *in vitro* on a bioabsorbable scaffold under aseptic conditions
- the source of the cells are foreskins from circumcised babies. Each foreskin can make more than 23,000 square metres of dermis
- as fibroblasts proliferate within the scaffold, they secrete human dermal collagen, matrix proteins and growth factors to form a human dermal tissue
- used as a permanent replacement dermis that provides a healthy wound bed which promotes epithelialization, resulting in faster healing of significantly more full-thickness (deep) diabetic foot ulcers
- recommended treatment regimen is one piece implanted in the ulcer weekly, until the ulcer is healed. In a large multicentre controlled study up to eight applications were used. Previously implanted tissue is NOT removed
- no allergic or immunological reactions have been reported to date
- should not be used in patients with known hypersensitivity to bovine serum albumin
- the product is manufactured, frozen and supplied within the protective confines of a bioreactor containing one piece of tissue measuring 5 x 7.5cm (2 x 3ins)
- the bioreactor is stored at −70°C and supplied in an insulated container packed with dry ice
- before application, the bioreactor is thawed, opened, and the dermal tissue is rinsed by a medical professional

- the ulcer is traced to allow sizing and shaping of the tissue to fit the wound bed which must meet the criteria for skin grafting
- The York Health Economics Consortium have estimated that at a cost of £250 per piece, Dermagraft is expected to reduce the annual cost per patient treated from £3,620 to £3,492 (a saving of £128 per patient)
- launched in the UK in October 1997 (current cost is £258.75 per piece)
- in June 1998, the FDA in the USA did not approve Dermagraft. The results of a new trial have been submitted for a new license application (August 2000)

DERMAL PADS (Spenco Medical UK)
- provide an extra layer of synthetic tissue protection that cushions and protects areas of the body which lack soft tissue padding, e.g. sacrum, heels, elbows
- absorb pressure and will help reduce the effects of both pressure and friction
- will naturally adhere to any skin surface and may be held in place by tape or bandage. They are NOT used as primary wound dressings
- can be easily cut and shaped to fit requirements and are re-usable

DESLOUGHERS AND CLEANSERS
see ASERBINE, CHLORAMINE, CHLORASOL, CHLORINATED SOLUTIONS, DAKINS', DEBRISAN, EUSOL, GRANUGEL, HIOXYL, HYDROCOLLOIDS, HYDROGEN PEROXIDE, INTRASITE GEL, IODOFLEX, IODOSORB, MILTON, NORMASOL, SODIUM CHLORIDE, SUGAR PASTE, VARIDASE[53]
- there is insufficient evidence to promote the use of one debriding agent over another[54]
- there is only a single comparison between two debriding agents that produced a significant result – Intrasite Gel significantly reduced necrotic wound area compared with dextranomer polysaccharide paste[49]

DRAWTEX (Activa Healthcare)
- a hydrocellular, 3-layer capillary dressing which is very absorbent
- outer layers are 100% polyester; inner layer consists of 30% polyester and 70% cotton fibres
- used for medium to heavily exuding wounds
- several layers of dressings can be used on most wounds
- available in 6 sizes

DRISORB (Vernon-Carus)
see NON/LOW-ADHERENT DRESSINGS
- low-adherent, absorbent dressing pad

- used as a secondary dressing in conjunction with a primary wound dressing

DUODERM
see GRANUFLEX, HYDROCOLLOIDS
- American/European form of Granuflex
- the Duoderm hydrocolloid dressings possess effective physical barrier properties to both HIV-1 and Hepatitis B virus when stringently challenged *in vitro*[55]

DUODERM EXTRA THIN (ConvaTec, DT)
see GRANUFLEX, HYDROCOLLOIDS
- thin, semi-permeable hydrocolloid dressing without adhesive border
- consists of an inner layer of hydrocolloids contained within an adhesive polymer matrix and an outer layer of polyurethane film
- used for acute and chronic lightly exuding wounds, e.g. post-operative sutured wounds, superficial pressure ulcers, abrasions
- particularly suitable in areas where movement is necessary because the dressing is highly flexible
- should not be left in place for longer than 7 days

DYES
- can be divided into five groups, the two main types being the acridine and triphenyl-methane derivatives which are bacteriostatic:
  1. Acridines e.g. acriflavine, proflavine
  2. Eosin 2% w/v – popular in Scotland
  3. Mercurochrome 1–2%
  4. Potassium permanganate 1:8000 to 1:10,000 e.g. Permitabs
  5. Triphenyl methanes e.g. brilliant green 0.5%; crystal violet (gentian violet) 0.5%; magenta; malachite green
- traditionally used for their antimicrobial activity and as astringents to dry up macerated skin around wounds
- modern use has declined because of the lack of information on their clinical effectiveness and fears about their detrimental effects on wound healing

EGG PRODUCTS
- the use of egg white has been specifically prohibited by the Department of Health since 1988. "Some nurses and midwives continue to use raw eggs on pressure sores, ulcers and babies' sore bottoms. SUCH PRACTICES SHOULD CEASE IMMEDIATELY"[56]

ENSURE-IT (Becton Dickinson UK distributed by Southern Syringe Services)
see VAPOUR-PERMEABLE FILMS

EOSIN
see DYES
- 2% w/v aqueous eosin paint; a colouring agent
- bacteriostatic and fungistatic solution with a very broad spectrum; Pseudomonas is not sensitive
- dries up the granulation edges of a wound if it is too liberally applied

EPIVIEW (ConvaTec, DT)
see VAPOUR-PERMEABLE FILMS
- sterile thin adhesive polyurethane film dressing consisting of a 0.025mm polyurethane film coated with 0.025mm acrylic adhesive
- permeable to oxygen and moisture vapour
- waterproof and provides a bacterial barrier
- has a low coefficient of friction to reduce shear and rucking
- used for minor wounds, with peripheral and central IV catheters (**ported EpiView**, 6 x 7cm) and as a secondary dressing. It may also be used to prevent skin breakdown from friction or from exposure to continuous moisture

ESSENTIAL OILS[57]
- Ylang Ylang, Wintergreen: in the management of pain
- Bergamot, St. John's Wort: in the management of odour
- St John's Wort, German chamomile: to promote granulation tissue
- Lavender, Roman chamomile: as an inflammatory agent
- Myrrh, Tea Tree: for wound cleaning

ETE (Mölnlycke)
see NON/LOW ADHERENT DRESSINGS
- pad of rayon wadding with rayon silk wound contact layer stitched in chequered pattern; apply shiny side to the wound

EUSOL (DT)
see CHLORINATED SOLUTIONS[58]
- Edinburgh University SOlution of Lime: solution of chlorinated lime and boric acid containing not less than 0.25% w/v available chlorine with a pH of 7.5–8.5

- used for infected, necrotic ulcers; has an effective action against bacteria such as staphylococcus and pseudomonas
- must be freshly prepared and has a two-week expiry
- there is a rapid inactivation of the antiseptic effect when contaminated by organic materials, e.g. pus and dressings
- caustic to ulcer and surrounding skin; destroys and damages healing tissue
- may cause the release of endotoxins from micro-organisms, e.g. coliforms. This may cause side effects ranging from mild uraemic toxaemia to serious renal failure (Schwartzmann reaction)
- may cause the formation of exuberant and excessive granulation tissue
- the addition of paraffin prevents dressing adherence and maintains a moist environment e.g. Eusol and Liquid Paraffin Emulsion
- Eusol, half-strength Eusol and Eusol and Liquid Paraffin Emulsion should not be used for wound care – disadvantages outweigh the benefits
- alternative agents are listed in the appendix – Management of wounds/wound types

EXU-DRY (S & N)
see NON/LOW ADHERENT DRESSING
- a multi-layered dressing consisting of:
  - a low adherent wound contact layer
  - an anti-shear layer to reduce pain and trauma
  - highly absorbent inner layers
  - semi-permeable outer layer
- indicated for a variety of wounds but targeted at burns
- available as dressings, sheets, garments,wound veils and pads

FLAMAZINE (S & N, POM)
see ANTIBACTERIALS and SILVER
- a hydrophilic cream containing silver sulfadiazine 1% w/w oil-in-water emulsion; also contains polysorbates, glycerol monoester, cetyl alcohol, liquid paraffin, propylene glycol and purified water
- topical broad-spectrum antibacterial; inhibits the growth of nearly all pathogenic bacteria and fungi *in vitro*
- used to treat a variety of wounds where infection may prevent healing e.g. leg ulcers, pressure ulcers, burns etc.
- marked antibacterial action against MRSA – 51 strains (100% effective), gentamicin-resistant pseudomonas (21 strains), gentamicin-resistant enterococci – (23 strains) and glycopeptide-resistant enterococci (54 strains)

- has achieved wide acceptance as the agent of choice for the prevention of Gram-negative sepsis in patients with extensive burns (first used in burns in 1968)
- antibacterial activity is prolonged because of the gradual release of silver ions which act on the bacterial cell surface to cause drastic alterations in the cell wall and plasma membrane
- mainly used under absorbent dressings which are changed daily (for burns) or at least three times a week (for leg ulcers)
- leucopenia has been reported in 3–5% of burns patients treated with cream
- sensitivity reactions occur uncommonly but the incidence is lower than with other sulphonamides; the vast majority of sensitisation reactions are due to one of the excipients in the cream
- use with caution if renal/hepatic function becomes impaired
- argyria has been reported[59] with excessive use (50g every 2 days for 5 months)
- cream should not be applied to skin surrounding the ulcer otherwise it may cause maceration
- in a prospective randomised trial, Mepitel reduces healing time in burned paediatric patients in comparison with silver sulfadiazine treatment[60]

FLEXI-BAN (Activa Health Care, DT)
- sub-compression wadding bandage

FLEXIPORE (Innovative Technologies, DT)
see FOAMS (formerly known as Spyroflex and Cliniflex)
- sterile, vapour-permeable dressing consisting of two layers:
  - Pressure-sensitive hydrophilic adhesive
  - Flexible microporous polyurethane membrane
- gas/moisture vapour permeable, yet provides an effective barrier to water/bacteria
- used for lightly exuding wounds, including minor trauma
- not recommended for use on grossly infected wounds
- should be changed on exuding wounds after seven days
- may be cut/overlapped if necessary
- manufactured by Innovative Technologies and distributed by Tissue Science Laboratories, Greyholme House, 49 Victoria Road, Aldershot, Hampshire GU11 1SJ

FOAM DRESSINGS
see ALLEVYN RANGE, ASKINA TRANSORBENT, BIATAIN, CAVI-CARE, FLEXIPORE, LYOFOAM, LYOSHEET, SPYROSORB AND TIELLE
- suitable for exuding flat and cavity wounds

FUCIDIN (Leo, DT, POM)
see ANTIBIOTICS
- available as ointment, gel and cream containing fusidic acid 2%. The ointment base contains lanolin
- topical use carries the risk of skin sensitisation
- not recommended for wound care

FUCIDIN INTERTULLE (Leo, DT, POM)
see ANTIBIOTICS
- sterile gauze squares each impregnated with sodium fusidate 2% (Fucidin ointment which contains lanolin)
- potent topical antibacterial agent with a narrow spectrum against Gram-positive bacteria and anaerobes
- bacterial resistance has been reported
- contact sensitisation may occur
- hypersensitivity reactions have been reported rarely
- not recommended for wound care

GELIPERM (Geistlich Pharma)
see HYDROGELS. Available as wet sheet and gel:
- **Wet Geliperm Sheet:** 96% water and a mixture of agar and polyacrylamide. It is impermeable to bacteria but permeable to water vapour and gases
- absorbent and may be used on lightly exuding wounds or dry wounds
- feels wet and cold on touch but is neither
- transparent so wound can be inspected if exudate is clear
- sometimes during application it becomes dry and brittle on a wound because of evaporation; rehydration may be necessary. It is a difficult dressing to handle
- on average needs changing every three days. Heavily exuding wounds may require to be changed daily. The dressing needs changing when it has become cloudy or opaque due to the absorption of wound exudate
- the results of a laboratory study suggest that Geliperm (and Vigilon) are likely to be ideally suited only to wounds that exude at a rate which is compatible with the fluid handling properties of the dressings[61]
- **Granulate Gel:** an agar-polyacrylamide gel containing 93.5% water which is able to absorb up to six times its own weight of exudate. It can be applied to deeper ulcers and cavities but is much more expensive than other gels

GRANEODIN (Squibb, POM, DT)
see ANTIBIOTICS
- ointment containing 0.25% neomycin and 0.025% gramicidin in Plastibase

- applied 2–4 times daily for a maximum of 7 days
- sensitivity to neomycin and gramicidin may occur
- ototoxicity and nephrotoxicity have been reported
- not recommended for wound care

GRANUFLEX (ConvaTec, DT)
see HYDROCOLLOIDS

- consists of an outer waterproof polyurethane foam, bonded onto a polyurethane film, which acts as a carrier for the hydrocolloid base. The base consists of gelatin, pectin, carboxymethylcellulose, adhesives and other polymers
- the hydrocolloids are held in a matrix which is cross-linked and this forms a stable mass in which the gel is contained
- used for light to medium exuding wounds
- dependent on exudate, the dressing can be left in place for up to seven days
- available as bordered and non-bordered dressings including triangular shapes which are specially designed to fit sacral pressure ulcers
- the hypoxic and acidic environment under the dressings encourages angiogenesis resulting in the development of healthy granulation tissue
- there is published evidence of resolution and prevention of fibrin clots under Granuflex
- Comfeel and Granuflex have been compared[47]
- in a randomised controlled clinical study comparing Tielle with Granuflex, Tielle was better in preventing leakage and reducing odour, but there were no differences in healing rates of patients with leg ulcers or pressure ulcers[62]
- in a randomised comparison comparing Allevyn Adhesive with Granuflex, the data indicate that both dressings are easy and convenient to apply; absorbency and ease of removal were better with Allevyn; wear times were similar[11]
- a chronic inflammatory reaction has been reported in full-thickness excised lesions on *porcine* skin. This appeared to be in response to particulate matter that had been incorporated into the wound bed and hypodermis, and was still apparent six months after injury, when hydrocolloid particles were detectable microscopically in the hypodermis[63]. A subsequent histological evaluation of chronic human wounds treated with hydrocolloid and non-hydrocolloid dressings showed no significant adverse histological sequelae[64]
- **Granuflex Paste:** for cavity wounds

GRANUFLEX Bordered (ConvaTec, DT)
see HYDROCOLLOIDS, GRANUFLEX

- border consists of an adhesive polyurethane foam which extends 2.0–2.5cm around area of hydrocolloid

- bordered version of Granuflex specifically designed to fit sacral and difficult to dress areas
- used for light to medium exuding wounds
- available in a range of sizes including square and triangular shapes

GRANUGEL (ConvaTec, DT)
see, HYDROCOLLOIDS, HYDROGELS
- a sterile, smooth, clear gel containing hydrocolloid powders. The gel consists of 80% water with sodium carboxymethylcellulose, pectin and propylene glycol (15%)
- gel is viscous with a slight adhesive tack allowing easy application
- indicated for deep and superficial wounds, dry, sloughy and necrotic wounds
- in dry conditions, the gel releases moisture, thus aiding the natural autolytic process. On moist wounds, the gel is capable of absorbing twice its weight in fluid
- gel is changed at intervals not exceeding three days when used on sloughy, necrotic wounds, or seven days on clean granulating wounds
- available in 15g single use tubes with sterile nozzle

GROWTH FACTORS (wound hormones)
see REGRANEX
- also known as Colony-Stimulating Factors, Cytokines and Interleukins
- includes cytokines and peptides of low molecular weight which act locally, having a specific high affinity for cell surface receptors and the ability to stimulate or inhibit cell proliferation or differentiation[65, 66, 67]
- over 30 growth factors (GFs) have been identified of three main types: proliferative (causing cell replication), migratory (chemoattractants which stimulate movement of cells) and transforming which produce a phenotypic alteration[68, 69]:
  - Epidermal GFs:
    - EGF: Epidermal GF (epithelialisation)
    - TGF-alpha: Transforming GF alpha (epithelialisation)
    - Heparin-binding epidermal GF
  - Fibroblast GFs:
    - FGF: Fibroblast GF (angiogenesis)
    - Acidic Fibroblast GF (angiogenesis and fibroblast proliferation)
    - Keratinocyte GF: (epidermal cell motiliy and proliferation)
  - Transforming GFs:
    - TGF-beta: Transforming GF beta (matrix synthesis)
  - Other GFs:
    - PDGF: Platelet-derived GF (angiogenesis, fibroplasia)

- VEGF: Vascular endothelial GF (angiogenesis)
- Tumour necrosis GF alpha
- 1L–1: Interleukin–1
- ILG–1: Insulin-like GF 1 (fibroplasia)
- M–CSF: Monocyte-colony stimulating GF (monocyte migration and maturation)
- GM–CSF: Granulocyte monocyte-colony stimulating GF (monocyte migration and maturation)

- clinical studies in the treatment of non-healing human wounds have reported disappointing results. GFs are destroyed by protein-degrading enzymes in the wound[70]

H–F ANTIDOTE GEL (IPS Health Care)

- contains Calcium Gluconate BP 2.5% in a clear, water-miscible gel base
- used as first-aid treatment of hydrofluoric acid burns to reduce burn damage to bone and deep tissue
- calcium gluconate combines with hydrofluoric acid to neutralise the fluoride ion

HAEMOSTATICS

see ALGINATES, OXYCEL, SURGICEL

- compounds used for the treatment or prophylaxis of haemorrhage by inhibiting the breakdown of the fibrin clot
- oxidised cellulose is an absorbable haemostatic which should not be used as a surface dressing, except for immediate control of bleeding as it inhibits epithelialisation
- some alginates are ideal for bleeding wounds

HAIR REMOVERS

- depilatory creams should be used rather than shaving which "nicks" the skin and may cause infection

HIOXYL CREAM (Quinoderm)

see HYDROGEN PEROXIDE SOLUTION

- a white, non-greasy cream containing stabilised hydrogen peroxide, 1.5% (equivalent to 5 volume hydrogen peroxide) of low pH
- gives a prolonged antiseptic action (for at least eight hours) which is a result of its steady release of oxygen when applied to tissues
- clinical experience indicates that the optimal dressing frequency for a sloughy wound is daily. Once cleansing has been established, application every other day or even every third day has been found to be acceptable

- may sting when applied
- do not mix with other topical medicaments likely to react with hydrogen peroxide

HONEY[71]

see SUGAR

- has been used in wound care since the time of the Ancient Egyptians when it was the most popular drug
- contains digested sugars (glucose and fructose), vitamins, minerals and enzymes
- will not support bacteria growth because of its high osmotic pressure
- antibacterial activity is due mainly to hydrogen peroxide which is liberated by an enzyme reaction. Some types of honey may also contain antibacterial substances derived from flowers visited by bees[72]
- has effective antibacterial, debriding and anti-inflammatory properties; acts as a stimulant for the growth of new blood capillaries, fibroblasts and epithelial cells[73, 74]
- randomised controlled trials have shown that in honey-dressed wounds, early subsidence of acute inflammatory changes, better control of infection and quicker wound healing was observed compared to silver sulphadiazine in controlling infection in burn wounds[75]
- honeys with an average level of antibacterial activity could be expected to be effective in preventing the growth of pseudomonads on the surface of a wound even if the honey were diluted more than ten-fold by exudation from the wound[76]
- is a viscous liquid which is difficult to retain in the wound; dressing pads pre-impregnated with honey are the most convenient method of applying honey to wounds (rather than directly to the wound)
- it is non-irritant and has a low pH
- do not use in diabetics: glucose and fructose can be absorbed from an open wound
- researchers at the University of Wales Institute are conducting trials on the use of absorbent pads impregnated with active Manuka honey from New Zealand. The dressings are irradiated and used to treat recurrent wound infections
- it is progressively diluted with exudate during use. This reduces its osmotic effect but other antimicrobial components in honey will ensure that inhibition is maintained[77]
- is prone to contamination with clostridial spores and non-pathogenic *Bacillus* spp.
- honey for clinical uses should be sterile and derived from specified pathogen-free hives, which have not been treated with drugs, and are gathered in areas where no pesticides are used[78]

HONEY, ANTIBACTERIAL (Medihoney)
see HONEY
- pure honey derived from selected *Leptospermum* spp.
- particularly effective against *Staphylococcus aureus* and *Pseudomonas* spp.
- available in 50g tubes
- further information is available on website: www.medihoney.com

HOSPI-FOUR (Millpledge Healthcare, DT)
see BANDAGES FOUR-LAYER

HYALOFILL (ConvaTec)
see HYALURONIC ACID
- composed of sterile 100% Hyaff biopolymer
- on contact with wound exudate, completely dissolves to form a thick hyaluronic acid-rich gel which promotes moist wound healing
- used for chronic wound management to promote granulation and contraction in recalcitrant wounds
- used until a healthy granulating wound bed has formed; once this phase has been initiated, moist wound dressings are used to complete wound closure
- depending on the level of exudate, lasts for up to 3 days
- can be cut without linting and can be folded to conform to the wound
- requires a secondary dressing
- 100% biodegradable
- available as fibrous sheets (10x10cm, 5x5cm) and ribbon (0.5g) – but not in DT

HYALURONIC ACID
see HYALOFILL, SEPRAFILM
- a major carbohydrate component of the extracellular matrix of skin, joints, eyes and most organs and tissues
- accelerates tissue repair by:
  - inducing a prompt angiogenic response
  - prompting rapid formation of granulation tissue
  - assisting fibroblast growth and movement
  - directing the organisation of collagen deposition

HYDROACTIVE DRESSINGS
see CUTINOVA CAVITY/HYDRO/FOAM/THIN
- manufactured from polyurethane matrix containing super-absorbent molecules
- selectively absorbs mainly water, leaving essential ingredients for wound healing on the wound bed (physiological cleansing of wound)

- used on exuding wounds from deep cavities to skin graft donor sites
- Cutinova foam/hydro/thin do not require secondary dressings
- does not adhere to wound bed
- no gel residue is left on wound bed, lessening the need for intensive irrigation
- recommended that dressings are changed within 2–3 days or sooner, depending on level of exudate. As healing proceeds, frequency of dressing change reduces
- remains stable when wet, making dressings easy to handle at dressing change
- molecular structure prevents squeeze out under compression
- some patients experience tingling sensation due to physiological debriding action

HYDROCOLL (Hartmann, DT)
see HYDROCOLLOIDS

- self-adhesive, absorbent hydrocolloid dressing covered with a semi-permeable polyurethane layer
- suitable for medium exuding wounds
- available in the Drug Tariff in a variety of sizes and shapes including presentations with bevelled edges to fit heels, elbows and sacral areas:
  - **Hydrocoll basic**
  - **Hydrocoll** – with bevelled edges
  - **Hydrocoll thin**
  - **Hydrocoll sacral** – shaped dressing with bevelled edges and flexible hinge
  - **Hydrocoll heel/elbow** – shaped dressing with bevelled edges

HYDROCOLLOIDS
see AQUACEL, ASKINA BIOFILM TRANSPARENT, COMBIDERM, COMFEEL, CUTINOVA, DUODERM, GRANUFLEX, GRANUGEL, HYDROCOLL, REPLICARE ULTRA, SUPRASORB H TEGASORB, ULTEC, VARIHESIVE[47, 79, 80]

- a hydrocolloid is a microgranular suspension of various natural or synthetic polymers, e.g. gelatin or pectin, in an adhesive matrix, e.g. polyisobutylene, the granules being in a semi-hydrated state and hydrophilic, and the adhesive matrix being of a hydrophobic nature. Standardisation of constituents may be a problem
- dressings should extend at least 2cm beyond the edge of the wound
- may release degradation products from the dressing into the wound[63]
- dressings are "interactive" in contact with wound exudate. Hydrocolloids slowly absorb fluid leading to a change in the physical state of the dressing, forming a gel which may be cohesive and/or hydrophilic

- provide an environment conducive to rapid debridement, thus there may be an initial increase in wound size
- when the hydrocolloid liquifies, it swells into the cavity and applies pressure to the base of the wound
- suitable for desloughing and for light to medium exuding wounds
- the manufacturers' recommendations should be followed when treating infected wounds. In a prospective trial, the risk of clinical infection is less under occlusive dressings such as hydrocolloids than under conventional impregnated gauze dressings (tulle gras) in small partial thickness burns, donor sites and venous leg ulcers[81]. A retrospective review shows similar results[82]
- the use of hydrocolloids in the treatment of diabetic foot has been reviewed[83]
- require no secondary dressing
- initially may need changing daily. Once the exudate has diminished, dressings may be left in place for up to seven days. Heavy exudate leads to too frequent changes of dressing
- dressings promote the formation of granulation tissue
- provide pain relief by keeping nerve endings moist
- In an *in vitro* assay, the hydrophilic particles of five hydrocolloid dressings significantly inhibited fibroblast proliferation[84]
- have barrier properties of varying degrees to gases, moisture vapour and micro-organisms
- are variably transparent/semi-transparent in use
- waterproof, so patient can bath or shower; the dressing should seal round the borders of a wound
- odour may be a concern with some dressings
- hydrocolloids have many of the characteristics of an ideal dressing (*see* appendix)
- available in different forms – wafers (thick and thin), granules, powders, gels and paste

HYDROFILM (Hartmann, DT)
see VAPOUR-PERMEABLE FILMS

HYDROGELS
see AQUAFORM, CLEARSITE, GELIPERM, GRANUGEL, HYDROSORB, HYPERGEL, INTRASITE, NORMLGEL, NOVOGEL, NU-GEL, OPRAGEL, PURILON, SPENCO 2ND SKIN, STERIGEL, SUPRASORB G, VIGILON
- available as flat sheets or amorphous gels having a high water content – gels are more commonly used

- cool the surface of the wound – this is said to be the cause of the marked reduction in pain. Products can be refrigerated to increase this effect
- suitable for desloughing and for light to medium exuding wounds
- contra-indicated where anaerobic infection is suspected – can support the growth of micro-organisms
- have a favourable permeability profile for gases
- some can act as a carrier for water soluble, topical medicaments
- some allow monitoring of the wound without disturbing the dressing
- sheet hydrogels may be used "cut-to-shape" of the wound or may overlap
- they do not swell into a wound like the hydrocolloids
- most hydrogels need a secondary dressing
- the results of a laboratory study suggest that Geliperm and Vigilon are likely to be ideally suited only to wounds that exude at a rate which is compatible with the fluid handling properties of the dressings[61]
- hydrogels have many of the characteristics of an ideal dressing (*see* appendix) but there may be some difficulties in application

HYDROGEN PEROXIDE SOLUTION
- usual strength of solution is 10 volume (3%)
- caustic effect on wounds in concentrations above 20 volume (6%)
- used to clean dirty, infected, necrotic, sloughy wounds but is not recommended on clean wounds
- contamination with organic material results in loss of effectiveness
- has an antiseptic effect due to its release of oxygen when applied to tissues – 1ml hydrogen peroxide 3% (10 volume) will release 10ml oxygen (oxidising agent)
- reacts with catalase causing frothing which helps to lift out foreign matter from the wound
- beware chemical interactions with other agents
- irrigation of hydrogen peroxide solution under pressure or into enclosed body cavities may have serious consequences such as oxygen embolus and surgical emphysema[85]. A patient died due to air embolism attributed to hydrogen peroxide[86]
- may be caustic to surrounding skin and wound[14, 87]
- at low concentrations, may stimulate fibroblast proliferation[88]. At concentrations recommended for wound cleansing, it produced 100% killing of all cell types[45]. Hydrogen peroxide fibroblast toxicity exceeds bacterial toxicity[14]. In an *in vitro* study, at concentrations that preserve fibroblast function, 0.003% hydrogen peroxide solution failed to reduce any bacterial counts[89]

HYDROSORB (Hartmann)
see HYDROGELS

- a sterile, transparent, self-adhesive hydrogel dressing consisting of 60% water and absorbent polyurethane polymers covered with a semi-permeable polyurethane film
- used for the treatment of slow-healing wounds, second-degree burns, abrasions and painful tissue injuries
- the upper surface of the dressing is marked with a grid to aid documentation of wound size
- the three-dimensional gel structure is not dissolved by absorbing wound exudate and thus can be removed from the wound in one piece without leaving any residue
- the gel has a slight cooling effect
- available in three sizes but not in the DT

HYDROSORB COMFORT (Hartmann)
see HYDROGELS and HYDROSORB

- has an additional hypoallergenic, broad, continuous adhesive border to ensure that the dressing stays in place
- available in three sizes but not in the DT

HYPERGEL (Mölnlycke)
see HYDROGELS

- 20% sodium chloride gel which hydrates and draws fluid from the wound
- used on dry necrosis

INADINE (J & J, DT)
see ANTISEPTICS, POVIDERM and POVIDONE-IODINE

- a sterile, low-adherent knitted viscous dressing impregnated with 10% povidone-iodine in a water-soluble polyethylene glycol base
- has been improved by increasing the loading of povidone iodine ointment and by reducing the number of threads
- dressing is now softer and more conformable
- may be used for prophylaxis and treatment of a wide range of bacterial, protozoal and fungal organisms in superficial burns and skin loss injuries
- the dressing should only be changed when the distinctive orange-brown colour changes to white; this indicates that the povidone-iodine has been used up
- the amount of free iodine available is very low but there may be some sensitivity to povidone-iodine or iodine
- not more than four dressings should be used at the same time

INDERMIL (Sherwood, Davis & Geck)
see ADHESIVES (TISSUE), DERMABOND
- contains N-butyl cyanoacrylate
- a translucent medical adhesive for closing wounds and lacerations
- cannula applicator available
- available as a unit dose (0.5g) and clinic kits (5g)

INSULIN
- topical insulin is effective in accelerating the healing of wounds in humans[90]
- this may be due to the insulin and/or to the zinc which it contains

INTERPOSE (Frontier Multigate)
see NON/LOW ADHERENT DRESSING
- range of absorbent dressing pads available

INTRASITE CONFORMABLE (S & N, DT)
see HYDROGELS and INTRASITE
- a non-woven dressing impregnated with Intrasite Gel
- used for dry, sloughy or necrotic wounds; lightly exuding wounds; granulating wounds
- facilitates the gentle packing of shallow or deep, awkwardly shaped or undetermined wounds
- secondary dressings are required
- range of product sizes available suitable for all wound sizes:
  - 10 x 10cm (7.5g loading)
  - 10 x 20cm (15g loading)
  - 10 x 40cm (30g loading)

INTRASITE GEL (S & N, DT)
see HYDROGELS; formerly known as Scherisorb
- 2.3% modified sodium carboxymethylcellulose (cross-linked) polymer, 77.7% water and 20% propylene glycol (humectant and preservative)
- cross-linked polymer helps the gel to remain in place in the presence of exudate
- propylene glycol may cause sensitisation and irritation in a small number of patients
- suitable for use at all stages of wound healing from debridement of necrotic tissue to formation of granulation tissue
- should be changed at least every one to three days
- in contact with a wound, the gel absorbs excess exudate and produces a moist environment over the surface of the wound

- can be used to soften and hydrate eschar by facilitating rehydration of the wound
- may be used where aerobic and anaerobic infection is present. For clinically infected wounds, the patient must be receiving systemic antibiotics and daily dressing changes
- use of the incorrect depth may cause some slight drying out of the gel at the edges
- the gel can be removed from the wound by irrigating with sterile sodium chloride 0.9% w/v; there may be some difficulty in doing this
- secondary dressings are required, e.g. low-adherent dressings, absorbent pads or vapour-permeable films
- N.B. product-drug interaction with povidone-iodine or iodine preparations
- in a randomised trial comparing Sterigel with Intrasite in the debridement of necrotic pressure sores, there were no significant differences in comfort, wound odour, surrounding skin condition or time to debridement[91]
- Intrasite Gel is more effective at promoting debridement than Debrisan Paste[49]
- Intrasite Gel and Debrisan Paste are both efficacious in the debridement of non-viable tissue. Intrasite Gel had a greater impact in reducing wound area; was superior in ease of application and removal, in reducing pain on application and removal; and in patient comfort during wear[50]
- Intrasite has enhanced fluid-absorbing properties but this has been achieved at the expense of the fluid-donating properties[92]
- sterile gel available pre-mixed in a unique applipak dispenser: 8g (DT), 15g (DT) and 25g

IOBAN 2 (3M)
see VAPOUR-PERMEABLE FILMS
- polymeric film coated with a hypoallergenic adhesive on one side in which an iodophor complex is incorporated
- specifically designed as a surgical, adhesive incise drape
- provides a sustained release of iodine to the skin surface throughout use
- not recommended for use in patients with known sensitivity to iodine

IODINE
see IODOFLEX, IODOSORB
- effective against Gram-positive and Gram-negative organisms, anaerobes, fungi and yeasts, protozoa and viruses
- disrupts cell proteins and lipid membranes
- application to large wounds or severe burns may produce systemic adverse effects such as metabolic acidosis, hypernatraemia and impairment of renal function

- regular use should be avoided in patients with thyroid disorders or those receiving lithium therapy
- may interfere with thyroid function tests
- many of the concerns about iodine are based on the toxicity of older formulations containing elemental iodine, or arise from *in vitro* studies which may not be relevant to *in vivo* situations. Newer preparations appear to be safe, have useful antimicrobial properties and may be effective for the debridement and treatment of a variety of wounds (report of a consensus meeting)[93]

IODOFLEX (S & N, P)
see IODINE, IODOSORB POWDER and OINTMENT
- units of sterile cadexomer iodine paste containing iodine (0.9% w/w) in an inert base. The units consist of the paste sandwiched in protective gauze
- units should be changed 2–3 times per week or when there is a loss of colour
- maximum single application is 50g; weekly maximum must not exceed 150g; treatment duration should not exceed three months
- used for the topical treatment of all types of chronic wounds
- CONTRAINDICATIONS, WARNINGS – *see* data sheet – the warning relating to the co-administration of Iodoflex and sulfafurazoles and sulphonylureas has now been removed
- available in 5g, 10g and a new 17g unit which can absorb 60ml exudate

IODOSORB POWDER (S & N, P)
see IODINE
- consists of hydrophilic beads of cadexomer impregnated with elemental iodine (0.9% w/w); cadexomer is a modified starch hydrogel
- the cadexomer absorbs exudate and forms a gel providing a moist protected environment which is conducive to wound healing. The iodine acts as an anti-infective against existing infection and prevents re-infection
- used to treat infected, medium to heavily exuding wounds
- dressings should be changed daily, or when all the beads have become saturated with wound exudate
- when the iodine has been used up, the colour changes from dark brown to white
- some patients have experienced a drawing sensation in the first hour of application
- cadexomer iodine must not be used in patients with known or suspected iodine sensitivity or thyroid disease
- if dressing dries out, saline or sterile water will wash the bulk of the dressing away. Because Iodosorb is biodegradable, any remaining Iodosorb can be left in the wound, therefore not requiring disturbance of newly-formed fragile tissue

- mild erythema without sensitisation has been reported
- available in sterile 3g sachets
- cadexomer iodine and dextranomer have been compared in the treatment of venous leg ulcers[94]

IODOSORB OINTMENT (S & N, P)
see IODINE
- similar product to Iodosorb Powder, except in an easier-to-use formulation with an ointment base of polyethylene glycol
- used to treat chronic, light to medium exuding leg ulcers
- the ointment is less likely to cause a drawing sensation than Iodosorb Powder, because the absorption is more gradual
- the dressing should be changed approximately three times per week or when the ointment has become saturated with exudate – indicated by a loss of colour
- available in 10g or 20g tubes for single use. Each 20g tube of ointment will absorb 60ml wound exudate

IRRICLENS (ConvaTec, DT)
see SODIUM CHLORIDE
- 0.9% w/v sodium chloride in a 240ml non-metered aerosol can (ozone friendly – the propellant is nitrogen)
- aerosol allows fingertip control of pressure and volume of saline; minimising wastage
- indicated for topical irrigation and cleansing of wounds; available on prescription
- each can should yield 12–15 uses of 15–20ml of saline

JELONET (S & N, DT)
see PARAFFIN GAUZE/TULLE GRAS
- an open-mesh leno gauze impregnated with white soft paraffin; a "normal loading" product containing 175–220gm^2
- available packed in tins or individually wrapped

KY LUBRICATING JELLY (J & J)
- sterile water soluble medical lubricant based on polyhydric alchohols and cellulose ether
- preservatives are hydroxybenzoates (tubes) and chlorhexidine gluconate (sachets)
- contra-indicated in patients with known sensitivity to the preservatives or propylene glycol

- in a randomised, double-blind, controlled trial, a comparison was made of the relative efficacy of using Varidase in KY Jelly or KY Jelly alone. The results suggest that KY Jelly may be a cost-effective alternative to the use of Varidase in KY Jelly[95]

KALTOGEL (ConvaTec, DT)
see ALGINATE DRESSINGS
- sterile, absorbent dressing consisting of non-woven calcium alginate (80%) and sodium alginate (20%) fibre
- manufactured from an alginate with a high mannuronic to guluronic acid ratio
- used in the management of medium to heavily exuding wounds
- rapidly forms a firm, soft gel on contact with wound exudate due to an ion exchange reaction
- applied directly to the wound and can be removed either with gloved fingers or by irrigation with saline as appropriate

KALTOSTAT (ConvaTec, DT)
see ALGINATE DRESSINGS
- a sterile, absorbent dressing of non-woven calcium (80%) and sodium (20%) alginate fibre available as a wound dressing or cavity dressing
- the calcium-sodium alginate combination affords quicker gelling than calcium alginate and needs less exudate or blood to trigger the gelling action. A strong viscous gel is produced
- manufactured from a selected species of brown seaweed (*Laminaria hyperborea*) that contains guluronic acid and mannuronic acid in the proportions of 2:1
- used in the management of bleeding and non-bleeding, heavily to medium exuding wounds
- ideal for bleeding wounds
- cut or fold dressing to shape of wound
- in a clinical comparison of Kaltostat Cavity Dressing and Sorbsan Packing and Ribbon, there was no significant clinical difference in analgesic requirements, mean pain scores or bacterial counts at each dressing change. Nursing staff favoured the handling properties of Sorbsan and its availability in two product sizes[13]
- in pilonidal sinus excision wounds, both Allevyn and Kaltostat were found to be easy to use, effective and acceptable to patients and clinicians[9]
- in a randomised trial comparing Aquacel with Kaltostat, the data suggest that Aquacel may have a significantly longer wear time and reduced frequency of dressing change in patients with exuding leg ulcers[21]

- **Kaltostat Cavity Dressing** (2g): available in the DT as a soft alginate rope for cavity wounds

KETANSERIN
- serotonin (5HT) blocking drug
- encouraging results have been reported in European trials of topical ketanserin ointment in healing of leg ulcers
- workers have suggested a dual action: stimulation of granulation and collagen production in the first few days and inhibition of myofibroblast contraction (so reducing the formation of hypertrophic scars)
- not yet licensed for topical use but the oral drug is on the market as an antihypertensive agent (Serepres) in Italy

K–FOUR (Parema, DT)
see BANDAGES FOUR-LAYER

K–PLUS (Parema, DT)
see BANDAGES (EXTENSIBLE)
- a light compression bandage (type 3a)
- for the treatment of venous leg ulcers, alone or as part of a multi-layer system. It may also be used for the application of light pressure for the reduction of oedema
- applied as a spiral or as a figure of eight. Offers controlled compression of approximately 18–20mmHg at the ankle and 12–15mmHg at the calf
- available in six sizes (two of them on DT)

K–SOFT (Parema, DT)
sub-compression wadding bandage

Larv E (Biosurgical Research Unit, SMTL)
see MAGGOTS
- sterile larvae (maggots) of the common greenbottle *Lucilia sericata*
- used to treat most types of sloughy, infected or necrotic wounds; also as an adjunct to surgery and to prepare wound sites for grafting
- reduce or eliminate odour and combat infection by ingesting and killing bacteria – including MRSA[96, 97]
- may also reduce wound pain and stimulate the formation of granulation tissue
- should be used within 8 hours of receipt
- applied using a dressing system that retains the maggots within the wound,

allows drainage of exudate and an adequate supply of oxygen to avoid suffocation[98, 99] (for further details *see* the data card)

- 1–5 containers are applied dependent on the size and condition of the wound. Each container contains approximately 150 sterile maggots priced £48 (January 2000)
- when first applied to a wound they are only 2–3mm long but may increase in size rapidly to 8–10mm when fully grown
- generally left on a wound for a maximum of 3 days; a few treatment cycles may be required
- should not be used in wounds that have a tendency to bleed easily, or be introduced into wounds that communicate with body cavities or any internal organs. Also, should not be applied close to any large blood vessels. Maggots are of limited value in wounds covered with hard black eschar
- subject to availability, treatment may be provided in hospital or the community
- are being assessed for their effectiveness by the International Biotherapy Society, (contact: John Church, Chairman IBS, Tel: 01628 522 668)
- in the first randomised controlled comparison, there was a significant improvement in the time required to debride varicose ulcers using larvae as compared to Intrasite[100]
- granted the Millennium Product Marque
- Contact details: Biosurgical Research Unit (SMTL), Princess of Wales Hospital, Coity Road, Bridgend CF31 1RQ (Tel: 01656 752820)

LYOFOAM (SSL, DT)
see FOAM DRESSINGS
- a neutral, polyurethane foam :
  - heat treatment of the wound contact surface renders it hydrophilic, absorbent and smooth
  - the rest of the foam is hydrophobic and non-absorbent
- the smooth, shiny side is placed directly onto the wound surface
- used for open, exuding wounds of light to medium exudate
- can be left on a moist wound for up to seven days depending on exudate production
- should not be left *in situ* for extended periods in dry, shallow wounds where drying exudate may produce adhesion between the dressing and the wound
- exudate is absorbed horizontally across the hydrophilic surface; once saturated, it will become visible along the edge of the dressing (lateral strike-through)
- since the untreated foam is hydrophobic, the exudate does not pass to the outer surface of the dressing
- has many of the characteristics of a modern wound dressing (*see* appendix)

LYOFOAM A (SSL)

see FOAM DRESSINGS, LYOFOAM

- polyurethane foam island dressing (no secondary dressings required)
- consists of a Lyofoam dressing covered by a layer of highly conformable, self-adhesive polyurethane foam, which is water resistant
- used for lightly exuding wounds
- there was no significant difference between Lyofoam A and NA dressing in a randomised controlled comparative study in grade II and III pressure sores[101]

LYOFOAM C (SSL, DT)

see DEODORISING DRESSINGS, FOAM DRESSINGS, LYOFOAM

- contains a layer of material impregnated with activated carbon between a standard Lyofoam dressing and a thin layer of polyurethane foam
- used for light to medium exuding wounds, especially those that are malodorous or infected
- exudate is absorbed horizontally across the hydrophilic surface; since the carbon layer is separated from the exudate by the hydrophobic layer, it remains dry and active throughout the life of the dressing
- no claim is made for the carbon to adsorb bacteria – because of the structure of the dressing, this is not possible
- can be used alone with the carbon (dark) side uppermost and the smooth shiny side in contact with the wound
- the use of secondary dressings will impair the effectiveness

LYOFOAM EXTRA (SSL, DT)

see FOAM DRESSINGS, LYOFOAM

- extra absorbent – particularly for heavily exuding wounds
- applied with the pink side facing upwards
- **Lyofoam Extra Adhesive:** also available
- **Lyofoam Extra T:** extra absorbent tracheostomy and cannular dressing

LYOFOAM T (SSL)

see FOAM DRESSINGS, LYOFOAM

- polyurethane foam tracheostomy and cannula dressing (9 x 6.5cm)
- made from Lyofoam with a special "cross cut" designed to fit closely around the tubes, cannulae or pins used in invasive medical procedures

LYOSHEET (SSL)

see FOAM DRESSINGS, LYOFOAM

- polyurethane foam sheet

- used as a replacement for conventional sheets to absorb exudate from severe burns
- also provides a soft padding for the patient to lie upon
- available in three, large sizes

M AND M TULLE (Malam)
see COD LIVER OIL AND HONEY TULLE

MAGGOTS
see Larv E
- infestation by maggots (or larvae) of the order Diptera is termed myiasis[102]
- invasion of tissues by maggots is commonly seen in tropical countries
- produce powerful proteolytic enzymes that breakdown sloughy and necrotic tissue which are ingested as a source of nutrient
- if left in the wound, maggots are effective in debriding the wound
- traditionally removed from infested wounds by using ether, chloroform, hydrogen peroxide or raw steak!
- The Wound Care Society have published an educational leaflet on the use of sterile maggots[103]
- larvae may not survive well in wounds containing residues of some hydrogel dressings[104]

MEDI-PREP (SSL)
see ANTISEPTICS
- used for general skin preparation; cleaning cuts, wounds and abrasions; hand disinfection
- single use sachets of 1% Cetrimide BP

MEFILM (Mölnlycke, DT)
see VAPOUR-PERMEABLE FILMS
- made of polyurethane coated with a polyacrylic adhesive
- the packaging has a grid system for mapping wound size
- available in four different sizes

MEFIX (Mölnlycke, DT)
- a permeable, apertured, non-woven, synthetic polyester fabric tape coated with a layer of polyacrylate adhesive
- provides secure fixation of dressings on difficult places e.g. elbows, knees, hips etc.

MELGISORB (Mölnlycke, DT)
see ALGINATE DRESSINGS
- sterile, non-woven dressing of 96% calcium and 4% sodium alginate made from brown seaweed
- used for medium to heavily exuding wounds
- available in three flat sizes (5x5cm, 10x10cm and 10x20cm) and one cavity size (3 pieces of 32cm)

MELOLIN (S & N, DT)
see NON/LOW ADHERENT DRESSINGS
- a low-adherent dressing combining a perforated polyester film wound contact layer, an absorbent 80% cotton / 20% viscose pad and a non-woven backing material
- the low-adherent plastic film side of the dressing – shiny, rough side – is placed on the wound
- performs best on light to medium exuding wounds; does not absorb excessive exudate which may cause maceration; the improved version of Melolin is 20% more absorbent
- there is some adherence to wounds because exudate may dry in the holes
- secondary dressings are needed, e.g. bandages or adhesive tapes

MELOLITE (S & N)
see NON/LOW ADHERENT DRESSINGS
- absorbent fabric pad covered on both sides by polyethylene net

MEMBRANES
see OMIDERM, SUPRASORB M, TEGAPORE.

MEPIFORM (Mölnlycke)
see SILICONE DRESSINGS
- a thin, conformable, self-adherent silicone gel sheet
- can be lifted from the skin without losing its adherent properties-allowing for easy re-application ('Safetac' technology)
- used to manage old and new hypertrophic and keloid scars. It may take from 3 months up to 1 year or more to improve an old scar. For prophylactic treatment, it can be used for 2–6 months depending on the condition of the scar
- dressing is worn 24 hours a day with daily inspection and washing of the skin. Normally can be used for 7 days or longer
- a waterproof dressing which can be worn during showering and bathing
- available in a range of three, neutral-coloured sizes which can be cut to size

MEPILEX (Mölnlycke, DT)
see NON/LOW ADHERENT DRESSINGS, SILICONE DRESSINGS
- a soft silicone wound contact dressing with polyurethane foam film backing
- indicated for non-exuding to heavily exuding wounds
- use with care in heavily bleeding wounds
- can be left in place for up to seven days depending on the wound condition

MEPITEL (Mölnlycke, DT)
see NON/LOW ADHERENT DRESSINGS, SILICONE DRESSINGS
- a sterile non-adhesive dressing made of a medical grade silicone gel bound to a soft and pliable polyamide net
- the netting spaces occupy 15% of the surface area and permit passage of exudate
- used for non-exuding to heavily exuding wounds (should be covered with a simple absorbent secondary dressing)
- can be left in place for up to seven days depending on the wound condition
- in a prospective randomised trial, Mepitel reduces healing time in burned paediatric patients in comparison with silver sulfadiazine treatment[105]

MEPORE (Mölnlycke, DT)
see NON/LOW ADHERENT DRESSINGS
- apertured, non-woven polyester fabric coated with a layer of polyacrylate adhesive with an absorbent wound pad
- a pliable, post-operative and absorbent dressing for surgical wounds

MEPORE ULTRA (Mölnlycke, DT)
see NON/LOW ADHERENT DRESSINGS
- a vapour-permeable adhesive film dressing with an absorbent pad
- similar to Opsite Plus (S & N)

MERCUROCHROME
see ANTISEPTICS, DYES
- mercurodibromofluorescein (an organic mercuric salt combined with fluorescein)
- usually based in alcohol which fixes skin cells and is toxic to wounds
- has the adverse effects of mercury
- dermatitis, hypersensitivity, toxicity to epidermal cells and cases of severe reactions have been reported
- only feebly active as a bacteriostatic agent
- as the hazards associated with the use of mercury compounds generally outweigh any therapeutic benefit, its clinical use should be abandoned

MESALT (Mölnlycke)

- an absorbent viscose/polyester non-woven dressing impregnated with sodium chloride
- indicated for the management of heavily exuding wounds in the inflammatory phase, including infected wounds
- should not be used in dry or low exuding wounds
- in contact with wound exudate, creates an hypertonic environment which absorbs the exudate together with bacteria and necrotic material from the wound
- available in three flat sizes (5x5cm, 7.5x7.5cm and 10x10cm) and one cavity size (2x100cm)

MESORB (Molnlycke, DT)

- highly absorbent cellulose dressing with a fluid-repellent backing
- used as a primary or secondary dressing for medium to heavily exuding wounds

METALLINE (Lohmann, distributed by Vernon Carus, DT)

- needle punched aluminised coating onto non-woven surface to allow fluid transmission
- the aluminium-coated side should be applied to the wound
- available as tracheostomy and drainage dressings (with pre-cut punch hole and slit)

METRONIDAZOLE

see ANABACT, ANTIBACTERIALS, METROTOP GEL, NEUTRATOP [106, 107]

- actively bactericidal against anaerobic bacteria and certain protozoa; there is also some evidence for an anti-bacterial effect in certain aerobic organisms
- anaerobic organisms associated with malodour include bacteroides, *Clostridium perfringens* and peptostreptococcus. Aerobic organisms which produce offensive wound odours are proteus, pseudomonas and klebsiella
- controlled studies have shown a correlation between a reduction in smell and the eradication of anaerobic infection. Unfortunately continuous therapy is required because the organisms soon regrow when treatment is stopped
- can be given systemically to remove odour (200–400mg eight hourly). However metronidazole can cause nausea and long-term use is associated with neuropathy. Also the patient cannot drink alcohol during treatment
- there is a possibility that metronidazole may be absorbed after topical application; topical treatment, however, avoids many of the unwanted systemic side effects
- not always well tolerated orally

- there is also a possibility that by using metronidazole topically, antibiotic resistance may be induced. Thus the use of topical metronidazole should be restricted to fungating, malodorous tumours only
- metronidazole gel has not been compared with tablets for efficacy, speed of action or patient preference[108]
- the switch from oral to topical metronidazole in the treatment of malodorous wounds seems to have occurred on the basis of few reliable data[109]
- brand prescribing is recommended for wound care to avoid confusion with acute inflammatory exacerbation of acne rosacea products which are considerably more expensive – Metrogel (Novartis), Noritate (Kestrel), Rozex (Stafford-Miller) and Zyomet (Goldshield)

METROTOP GEL (SSL, POM)
see ANTIBACTERIALS, ANABACT, METRONIDAZOLE, NEUTRATOP
- clear, colourless gel containing metronidazole BP 0.8% w/v in an aqueous hypromellose base with Benzalkonium Chloride Solution BP 0.02% v/v
- the indications have been extended to the treatment of malodorous fungating tumours, leg ulcers and pressure sores
- use once or twice daily as necessary. Cavities should be loosely packed with paraffin gauze smeared in the gel
- can be re-used for single patient use for up to 28 days
- available in sizes 15g, 30g and 60g

MICRODON (3M)
- a sterile, soft-cloth wound dressing with an adhesive border
- absorbs exudate but resists wound adherence
- indicated for surgical incisions, cuts, abrasions and light to medium draining wounds
- available in a range of sizes from 5 x 7cm to 9 x 35cm

MILTON (Proctor and Gamble)
see CHLORINATED SOLUTIONS
- a stabilised 1% sodium hypochlorite solution
- when diluted 1 in 4, the solution contains 0.25% w/v available chlorine with a pH of 10.5–11.2 and is stable for several months

MULTIDRESS PRODUCTS (ConvaTec)
- a comprehensive range of sterile, general use dressings that provide a modern alternative to traditional products e.g. gauze
- should not be used for longer than 7 days

- reduced adherence to the wound
- **Multidress Compress:** a four-ply, non-woven absorbent dressing (10 x 10cm) containing gelling fibres for the management of exuding acute and chronic wounds
- **Multidress Standard:** an open knit absorbent dressing (10 x 10cm) containing gelling yarns for the management of exuding shallow or cavity acute and chronic wounds
- **Multidress WCL:** a non-adherent wound contact layer (10 x 10cm) containing gelling yarns for the management of acute and chronic wounds
- **Multidress Ribbon:** a packing strip (1.25cm x 5m) containing gelling yarns for the management of exuding cavity wounds, fistulae and sinuses
- **Multidress Extra:** an absorbent primary or secondary dressing (5 x 5cm, 10 x 10cm and 10 x 20cm) containing materials that actively absorb exudate for the management of light to medium exuding acute and chronic wounds. Place the shiny film side of the dressing in contact with the wound or primary dressing
- **Multidress Pad:** an absorbent secondary dressing (9 x 11cm, 9 x 17cm) for the management of medium to heavily exuding acute and chronic wounds. Place the white side of the dressing in contact with the primary dressing

MULTISORB (S & N)
- highly absorbent dressing pads

MUPIROCIN
see BACTROBAN

N-A. DRESSING (J & J, DT)
see NON/LOW ADHERENT DRESSINGS
- sterile, knitted, viscose primary dressing
- no loose fibres
- knitted open structure allows free passage of exudate through to secondary dressings
- has been improved by reducing the number of threads – dressing is now softer and more conformable

N-A ULTRA (J & J, DT)
see NON/LOW ADHERENT DRESSINGS, SILICONE DRESSINGS
(formerly called Silicone N–A)
- sterile silicone-coated knitted viscose dressing
- silicone coating is claimed to produce a non-adherent (rather than low-adherent) dressing

- silicone coating does not occlude the pores of the knitted fabric, thereby allowing drainage of exudate
- secondary dressings can be changed independently leaving N–A Ultra in position for up to 7 days

NEUTRATOP (S & N, POM)
see ANABACT, ANTIBACTERIALS, METROTOP, METRONIDAZOLE
- a transparent gel containing 0.75% metronidazole
- for the treatment of anaerobic infection in malodorous fungating topical tumours
- must be discarded after single use

NON/LOW-ADHERENT DRESSINGS
see CUTILIN, MELOLIN, RELEASE, SKINTACT, SOLVALINE N (absorbent, perforated plastic film-faced dressings)
see COSMOPOR E, MEPORE, PRIMAPORE, STERIFIX (absorbent, perforated dressing with adhesive border)
see N-A, N-A ULTRA, PARATEX, SETOPRIME, TRICOTEX (knitted viscose primary dressing)
see MEPITEL, MEPILEX (soft silicone wound contact dressings)
see also ALLDRESS, CUTICERIN, CUTIPLAST, DRISORB, ETE, INTERPOSE, MELOLITE, PRIMARY, TELFA
- most are low-adherent, rather than non-adherent
- can be used on their own on dry wounds or lightly exuding wounds. A secondary dressing is required when used to dress more heavily exuding wounds
- needs to be secured with bandages or adhesive tapes

NORMASOL (SSL, DT)
see SODIUM CHLORIDE
- 25ml and 100ml sterile sachets, containing 0.9% w/v sodium chloride solution
- sachets are not as user friendly as steripods

NORMLGEL (Mölnlycke)
see HYDROGELS
- 0.9% sodium chloride gel
- used to hydrate dry wounds and to debride sloughy and necrotic wounds

NOVOGEL (Ford Medical Associates, DT)
see HYDROGELS
- a glycerine based hydrogel sheet available in squares, rectangles and circulars

- consists of 65% glycerine, 17.5% polyacrylamide, 17.5% water with an outer covering of a breathable fabric
- used for dry "sloughy" or necrotic wounds; lightly exuding wounds; granulating wounds
- not suitable for infected or heavily exuding wounds
- care is needed to choose the appropriate secondary dressing
- will absorb 3–4 times its own weight
- **Elastogel:** similar product available in the USA

NOXYFLEX S (Geistlich Pharma, P)
- 1–2.5% solutions of noxythiolin in saline or water are sometimes used on infected wounds and burns
- potent antibacterial and antifungal activity
- exerts its effects via provision of a methylol radical
- acquired resistance does not occur and patient sensitisation is avoided
- mild discomfort on application may be relieved by addition of 2% lignocaine
- incompatible with iodine derivatives and hypochlorites

NU-GEL (J & J, DT)
see ALGINATES AND HYDROGELS
- 97% hydrogel with 3% sodium alginate
- indicated for sloughy and necrotic wounds and for moist wound healing
- maintains its consistency for up to three days on the wound
- available in a 15g concertina pack

OMIDERM (distributed by Iatro Medical Systems)
see MEMBRANES
- a non-adhesive dressing of polyurethane, bonded with hydrophilic monomers; relatively inelastic when dry but upon absorption of water it becomes elastic and conforming
- can be used for superficial and partial thickness burns, abrasions and on donor sites after haemostasis has been achieved. It can also be used in a number of other granulating wounds
- not recommended for use on infected, bleeding or heavily exuding wounds; on full thickness wounds, it is only recommended as a temporary dressing
- allows up to 5L fluid transport/square metre/24 hours
- as normal healing proceeds, Omiderm peels off the healed area and should be carefully trimmed to provide a 1cm border around the wound margin. If left undisturbed it will separate spontaneously from a healed wound once epithelial cover is achieved

- membrane shrinkage and wrinkling may be a problem
- the wound site protected with Omiderm should not be immersed or heavily wetted as this may cause removal of the dressing
- dressing changes are generally not necessary unless the wound shows signs of infection, fluid accumulation, haematoma or until final peel-off. Dressing life may be up to 20 days
- the dressing is removed by wetting with sterile saline or water
- antibacterials applied to the external surface will penetrate the membrane to reach underlying tissue. However, the integrity of the membrane is lost after three days on application of silver sulphadiazine[110]
- should not be used on patients with known sensitivity to polyurethane
- available in meshed and unmeshed varieties

OPRAFLEX (Lohmann, distributed by Vernon Carus)
see VAPOUR-PERMEABLE FILMS
- specially designed backing material acts as an application aid and ensures accurate, wrinkle-free placement

OPRASKIN (Lohmann, distributed by Vernon Carus)
see COLLAGEN
- a sterile collagen sponge: 1cm^2 and 0.8cm thick contains 7.3mg collagen (from young calf skins) and 0.42mg (maximum) hydrogen peroxide
- used for wounds with extensive tissue damage; sponge is cut to the size and shape of the wound (and moistened before application to dry wounds)
- dressings on infected wounds are changed daily; on heavily exuding wounds – daily or several times a day; on other wounds – the dressing can be left until healed and soaked off
- contra-indicated in heavily suppurating wound cavities
- interacts with chlorine-releasing antiseptics, with albumin-precipitating substances (silver nitrate) and with caustics (iodine tincture) which denature proteins
- sponges are available in various sizes

OPSITE FLEXIGRID (S & N, DT)
see VAPOUR-PERMEABLE FILMS
- consists of a film supported on a removable flexible carrier
- film is a thin, polyurethane layer coated with a hypo-allergenic acrylic adhesive
- flexible carrier incorporates a grid system for mapping wound size (including surface area)
- can be left in place for up to 14 days

OPSITE I.V. 3000 (S & N)
see OPSITE, VAPOUR-PERMEABLE FILMS
- consists of reactic hydrophilic polyurethane film coated with a water-based hypo-allergenic acrylic adhesive
- has a very high moisture vapour permeability which is 3 to 8 times more permeable to water vapour than conventional films
- specifically designed for intravenous catheter care

OPSITE PLUS (S & N, DT)
see VAPOUR-PERMEABLE FILMS, OPSITE
- vapour-permeable adhesive film dressing with absorbent pad

OPSITE POST-OP (S & N, DT)
see VAPOUR-PERMEABLE FILMS, OPSITE
- Opsite film combined with a low-adherent pad
- a waterproof bacteria-proof adhesive island dressing
- used for low to medium exuding wounds

OPSITE SPRAY DRESSING (S & N)
see BARRIER FILMS
- an acrylic copolymer, acetone/ethyl acetate spray containing no CFC propellants
- spray forms a transparent and quick-drying film which is permeable to moisture vapour and air; film can be peeled off when completely dry, left to slough off unaided or removed with adhesive plaster remover
- used for a variety of minor wounds, e.g. minor cuts, abrasions and sutures

OXERUTINS (Paroven, Novartis)[111]
- licensed for "relief of symptoms of oedema associated with chronic venous insufficiency"
- evidence for the efficacy of Paroven remains unconvincing, except in lymphoedema
- for those with severe symptoms of oedema, who do not tolerate, or who get insufficient relief from support stockings, Paroven may be worth trying for four weeks, but it should be continued only if it has clearly helped
- in lymphoedema, full doses definitely seem worth trying for six months

OXYCEL (Associated Hospital Supply)
see HAEMOSTATICS
- sterile oxidised cellulose

OXYGEN
- has been used to facilitate wound healing
- good results were obtained with arterial leg ulcers when periods of hyperbaric oxygen were interspersed with periods of tissue hypoxia when oxygen therapy was withheld[112]
- supplemental oxygen given during and after colorectal resection reduces the incidence of surgical wound infection by half[113]

PARAFFIN GAUZE / TULLE GRAS (non-medicated)
see JELONET, PARANET, PARATULLE, PERITEX, UNITULLE
- bleached cotton/rayon cloth impregnated with white or yellow soft paraffin (tulle gras equivalent to "greased net")
- dressings contain different weights of paraffin per unit area e.g.
  - Paranet (Light loading, 90–130g/m^2)
  - Jelonet (Normal loading, 175–220g/m^2)
- Paraffin reduces the adherence of the dressing to the wound if applied in sufficient thickness
- antibacterials can be dispersed in the soft paraffin but water-soluble medicaments may not be readily released into the wound; this results in variable efficacy
- requires secondary dressings, e.g. absorbent pads
- said to be semi-permeable and non-adherent but there may be some adherence due to the sticky nature of the paraffin which is difficult to remove from the wound with aqueous wound cleansing agents
- needs frequent changing to avoid drying out and incorporation in granulation tissue
- used as a primary wound dressing for clean, superficial wounds, e.g. abrasions, cuts or partial thickness burns

PARANET (Vernon-Carus, DT)
see PARAFFIN GAUZE/TULLE GRAS
- light loaded with paraffin, 90–130g/m^2, (sachets)
- normal loaded with paraffin (tins)

PARATEX (Parema, DT)
see NON/LOW ADHERENT DRESSINGS
- a non/low-adherent dressing similar to N-A, N-A Ultra, Setoprime, Tricotex
- a knitted viscous primary dressing

68

PARATULLE (SSL, DT)
see PARAFFIN GAUZE / TULLE GRAS
- sterile Paraffin Gauze Tulle Dressing BP
- a leno gauze impregnated with yellow soft paraffin
- a "light loaded" product containing 90g to 130g of paraffin base per square metre of cloth
- available individually wrapped and can be cut to shape before removing backing

PAROVEN (Novartis)
see Oxerutins

PASTE BANDAGES (DT)
- medicated paste bandages are used in the treatment of skin conditions associated with leg ulcers, e.g. eczema, inflammation
- are applied from the base of the toes to the tibial tuberosity (with the foot at right angles); additional bandaging is always required
- can be left *in situ* for 1 – 2 weeks before a further dressing is required; act as a buffer between the fragile, inflamed skin and the turns of the compression bandage
- are able to absorb exudate
- many patients are sensitive to some of the constituents of paste bandages such as parabens preservatives, lanolin, etc. It is advisable before using paste bandages, to patch test the patient with a small strip of bandage to the leg for at least 48 hours
- paste bandages are occlusive bandages which may increase absorption of topical medicaments, e.g. steroids
- there are many types of paste bandage available, all of which are available on DT (individually wrapped, 7.5cm x 6m):-

Zinc Paste Bandages
- bandages of choice for patients who display multiple sensitivities
- protective, soothing applications for reddened, irritated skin
- **Steripaste, (SSL, DT)** consists of an open-wove bleached cotton bandage impregnated evenly with a paste of zinc oxide 15% w/w. Also contains glycerol, coconut oil, aluminium magnesium silicate, xanthan gum, polysorbate 80, sorbitan-mono-oleate, synthetic spermaceti and purified water. Unique preservative-free formulation. A patch test study has not shown any convincing allergic reactions. It should be used cautiously in patients allergic to cetylstearyl alcohol and avoided in those allergic to a sorbitan ester[114]

- **Viscopaste PB7 (S & N, DT)** consists of an open-wove bleached cotton bandage impregnated evenly with a paste containing zinc oxide (10%), glycerol, cetostearyl alcohol, cetomacrogol, white oil, guar gum, xanthum gum, methyl and propyl parabens preservatives and water
- when compared to Kaltostat and a zinc oxide-impregnated stockinette, Viscopaste significantly improved the healing of chronic venous ulcers when used in combination with compression bandaging[115]
- **Zincaband (SSL, DT)** consists of an open-wove bleached cotton bandage impregnated evenly with a paste of zinc oxide (15%), modified starch, glycerine, castor oil, citric acid, hydroxybenzoate and water.

Zinc paste and calamine bandage
- action is mainly emollient: soothes irritated, fragile skin surrounding ulcer, e.g. erythema, eczema and dermatitis
- **Calaband (SSL, DT)** consists of an open-weave bleached cotton bandage impregnated evenly with a paste of zinc oxide (9.25%), calamine, modified starch, citric acid, glycerine, castor oil, phenosept and water

Zinc paste, calamine and clioquinol bandage
- action is anti-bacterial and deodorant
- suitable for grossly infected, offensive ulcers
- **Quinaband (SSL, DT)** consists of an open-wove bleached cotton bandage impregnated evenly with a paste of zinc oxide (9.25%), clioquinol (1%), calamine (5.75%), modified starch, citric acid, glycerine, castor oil, teepol, phenoxyethanol and water. Clioquinol is a broad-spectrum antibacterial agent of low sensitising potential. Use of Quinaband may result in elevation of serum protein-bound iodine levels

Zinc paste and coal tar bandage
- during normal treatment granulation will occasionally cease; short-term use of this bandage will often restart the process
- has anti-inflammatory and mild antiseptic properties
- used for dry and scaly skin, e.g. eczema, dermatitis, lichenification
- **Coltapaste (S & N, DT)** consists of an open-wove bleached cotton bandage impregnated evenly with a paste consisting of zinc oxide (15%), coal tar (3%), purified water, emulsifying wax, anhydrous lanolin, and methyl and ethyl parabens preservatives
- **Tarband (SSL, DT)** consists of an open-wove bleached cotton bandage impregnated evenly with a paste of zinc oxide (15%), coal tar (3%), glycerine, propyl hydroxybenzoate, modified starch, castor oil and water

Zinc paste and ichthammol bandages
- action is mainly anti-inflammatory
- may irritate or sensitise skin
- used to soothe irritated skin, e.g. eczema, when tar is not tolerated
- **Icthaband (SSL, DT)** consists of an open-wove bleached cotton bandage impregnated evenly with a paste of zinc oxide (15%), ichthammol (2%), modified starch, glycerine, castor oil, citric acid, propyl hydroxybenzoate and water
- **Ichthopaste (S & N, DT)** consists of an open-wove bleached cotton bandage impregnated evenly with a paste consisting of zinc oxide (6%), ichthammol (2%), glycerin, gelatin, cyclonette wax and phenoxetol

PENTOXIFYLLINE (Trental, Borg)[116]
- improves the delivery of oxygen in ischaemic tissues, has fibrinolytic effects that are possibly mediated by leucocytes, and reduces the adhesion of polymorphonuclear leucocytes
- these properties might explain the clinical benefit of pentoxifylline when added to a standard regimen of dressing and compression bandaging in increasing the healing rates of resistant venous ulcers. Treatment may need to be continued for several months.
- appears to be an effective adjunct to compression bandaging for treating venous ulcers. In the absence of compression, may be effective for treating venous ulcers. The majority of adverse effects are likely to be tolerated by patients, and gastrointestinal disturbances (indigestion, diarrhoea and nausea) are the most frequent[117]
- the difference in the healing rates of venous leg ulcers between patients taking pentoxifylline and placebo did not reach statistical significance[118]

PERITEX (Southon-Horton)
see PARAFFIN GAUZE / TULLE GRAS

PERMITABS (Bioglan)
see POTASSIUM PERMANGANATE
- purple, bi-convex, soluble tablets containing Potassium Permanganate BP 400mg
- a quantity of the required strength of solution may be prepared by dissolving the appropriate number of tablets in warm water, e.g. 1 tablet dissolved in 4 litres of water provides a 0.01% (1 in 10,000) solution
- the tablets should be handled as little as possible to avoid staining the fingers
- avoid getting the solution into the eyes, nose or mouth

PHENOXYETHANOL
see ANTISEPTICS
- is effective against strains of *Pseudomonas aeruginosa* but is less effective against other Gram-negative and Gram-positive organisms
- may be used as a 2% aqueous solution or cream

PHENYTOIN
- has been used in the healing of pressure sores, venous stasis and diabetic ulcers, traumatic wounds and burns[119] and large abscess cavities[120]. All the studies have reported enhancement of wound healing, with insignificant adverse effects
- phenytoin reduces oedema and inflammation, separates slough and accelerates the growth of granulation tissue. Phenytoin may promote wound healing by a number of mechanisms, including stimulation of fibroblast proliferation, facilitation of collagen deposition, glucocorticoid antagonism and antibacterial activity[119]
- patients receiving topical phenytoin should be monitored for signs of systemic toxicity as measurable phenytoin plasma concentrations are obtained

POLYSKIN II (Kendall)
see VAPOUR-PERMEABLE FILMS

POLYVINYLCHLORIDE FILM
see VAPOUR-PERMEABLE FILMS
- plasticised, thin, clear, sheeting that was originally produced for wrapping foodstuffs (as Clingfilm, Wrapfilm, etc.)
- cheap, easy to apply, comfortable to wear, pain-free to remove and transparent
- non-sterile
- has been used in burns units for dressings before the ward round, before surgery and when the patient is transferred from casualty to the burns unit

POTASSIUM PERMANGANATE
see DYES, PERMITABS
- stains the skin brown
- daily 15 minute soaks are used as an astringent in concentrations of 1 in 8000 to 1 in 10,000 to cleanse and deodorise suppurating eczematous wounds and acute dermatoses

POVIDERM (SSL, DT)
see ANTISEPTICS and POVIDONE-IODINE
- a sterile, knitted, viscous dressing impregnated with povidone-iodine fabric ointment 10% w/w (similar to Inadine)
- used for topical treatment of infection in minor cuts and abrasions and small areas of burns, including treatment of infection in decubitous and venous ulcers
- in use, colour changes from orange to white indicating that dressing should be changed

POVIDONE-IODINE
see ANTISEPTICS, BETADINE, INADINE, POVIDERM, SAVLON DRY, VIDENE
- an iodophore which is a loose complex of iodine and a carrier – povidone
- iodine is gradually released from the iodophore and has the broadest spectrum of activity of any antiseptic commonly available. In a comparative trial against 33 strains of methicillin resistant *Staph. aureus* (MRSA), chlorhexidine achieved full efficacy against only three strains of MRSA, whilst povidone-iodine was fully effective against every single strain on trial[39]
- has largely displaced the numerous antibiotic-containing ointments
- because of the slow release, povidone-iodine is less potent and less toxic than preparations containing free iodine
- in both an experimental and clinical study, povidone iodine did not cause any adverse reactions or have an adverse affect on wound healing[121]
- allergic contact dermatitis and one case of anaphylaxis have been reported[122]
- avoid use on large wounds as excessive absorption of iodine may occur
- antibacterial effect is reduced by contact with pus and exudate so the preparations must be applied at intervals sufficiently short for brown coloration to persist. Active iodine is brown; on inactivation, iodine is converted to colourless iodides
- does not cause permanent staining to skin or clothes
- alcoholic solutions should not be used
- its use has been extensively reviewed[123, 124, 125, 126]. Its therapeutic benefit in open wounds has been supported in some reviews but questioned by others because of delayed wound healing and iodine toxicity

PRIMAPORE (S & N, DT)
see NON/LOW ADHERENT DRESSINGS
- absorbent, perforated dressing with a Melolin-like low-adherent absorbent pad and an adhesive border

- indicated for post-operative use and also for cuts, lacerations and sutured wounds

PRIMARY (Robinson)
see NON/LOW ADHERENT DRESSING
- knitted viscous primary dressing
- available in 9.5 x 9.5cm and 12.5 x 14.5cm sizes

PROFLAVINE (DT)
see ANTISEPTICS
- an acridine derivative available as:
  - Proflavine solution – 0.1% aqueous solution of proflavine hemisulphate
  - Proflavine Cream BPC – 0.1% water in oil (w/o) emulsion containing wool fat
  - Proflavine Cream – 0.1% oil in water emulsion (o/w)
- slow-acting antiseptic ; mildly bacteriostatic against many Gram-positive bacteria but less effective against Gram-negative organisms e.g. *Proteus* spp., *Pseudomonas* spp. and *Escherichia coli*
- hypersensitivity reactions have been reported occasionally (the cream contains wool fat, a known sensitising agent)
- a w/o proflavine cream has little or no antibacterial activity as the proflavine is not released from the emulsion base; o/w emulsions should overcome this problem[127]
- proflavine creams do not offer any advantages over more modern alternatives. Calcium alginate (Sorbsan) is superior to traditional gauze soaked in proflavine in acute surgical wounds and abscesses in terms of comfort of dressing and bacterial clearance[128]

PROFORE (S & N, DT)
see BANDAGES (FOUR-LAYER)

PRO-TEX (Medical Agency Services)
- a non-woven three-layer non-adherent capillary dressing which is very absorbent
- consists of 100% polyester outer layers with a support surface of 65/35% polycotton
- inner and outer layers combine to lift and transport exudate and debris away from the wound surface
- absorbs up to 32 times its own weight
- several layers of dressings can be used on most wounds

- a 'drain pouch' is being developed
- due to be launched in Autumn 2000

PURILON GEL (Coloplast, DT)
see ALGINATES and HYDROGELS
- a hydrogel/alginate gel consisting of calcium alginate, CMC and more than 90% water
- primarily used for dry and moist necrotic wounds. Can also be used as a supplement to moist wound healing in general
- hydrates necrotic tissue and effects debridement
- absorbs debris and excess exudate
- requires a secondary dressing on top of the gel
- gel changing interval may be up to 3 days

REGRANEX (Janssen-Cilag, POM)
see GROWTH FACTORS
- clear, colourless to straw-coloured gel containing becaplermin 100µg/g (0.01%)
- a recombinant human platelet derived growth factor-BB (rhPDGF–BB)
- promotes the chemotactic recruitment and proliferation of cells involved in wound repair – the predominant effect is to enhance the formation of granulation tissue
- used for full thickness, neuropathic, chronic, diabetic ulcers less than or equal to 5cm^2
- applied once daily as a continuous thin layer to the entire ulcerated area and covered by a moist saline gauze dressing (not occlusive dressings)
- therapy should be continued to a maximum of 20 weeks as long as healing progress is seen on periodic evaluations
- contra-indicated for known hypersensitivity to any ingredient e.g. parabens preservatives, or for known neoplasm at or near the site of application (as becaplermin is a growth factor)
- use within six weeks after first opening
- store in the refrigerator at 2–8°C (do not freeze)
- safety and effectiveness have not been established in children and adolescents below the age of 18 years
- side effects reported in clinical trials: infection, skin ulceration, skin disorder, including erythema and pain, bullous eruption and oedema
- the net price is £275 for a 15g tube – a course of treatment is likely to cost between £550 and £825

RELEASE (J & J, DT)
see NON/LOW ADHERENT DRESSINGS
- low adherent ethylene methyl acrylate film wrapped around an absorbent core of viscose rayon sandwiched between two layers of non-woven fabric
- used for low to medium exuding wounds
- highly conformable

REPLICARE ULTRA (S & N, DT)
see HYDROCOLLOIDS
- used for light to medium exuding wounds
- available as square and anatomically shaped sacral, thin dressings

REPOSE (Frontier Therapeutics)
- The University Hospital of Wales, Cardiff have developed the **Repose** system of mattresses and cushions to prevent pressure sores
- utilises high-tech materials in a low-tech manner at low cost
- products are packed inside a pump which enables them to be easily inflated and ready for use within seconds

ROEHAMPTON BURNS DRESSING (Relyon)
- sterile first-aid foam dressing for application to burned areas, to protect against additional trauma and contamination and to provide protection in transit
- indicated for 1st, 2nd and 3rd degree burns

SALINE STERIPOULES (Bartholomew Rhodes)
see SODIUM CHLORIDE
- sterile sodium chloride 0.9% solution (20ml)

SAVLON DRY POWDER (Novartis)
see ANTISEPTICS and POVIDONE-IODINE
- 1.14% povidone-iodine dry powder spray in an aerosol

SAVLON WOUND WASH (Novartis)
- a ready to use, alcohol-free, antiseptic first-aid spray
- the pump spray delivery makes it ideal for cleansing minor wounds quickly

SEASORB (Coloplast, DT)
see ALGINATES – formerly called Comfeel Seasorb
- a xerogel of calcium alginate (92%) and sodium alginate (8%)

- used for highly exuding wounds
- the freeze-drying of alginate results in a highly porous fibre-free material, and therefore the dressing leaves no fibre in the wound
- the dressing remains intact after absorbing exudate because of a mesh net in the centre of the dressing
- available as a dressing and a rope filler (40cm/2g). The filler can be soaked in saline solution prior to application

SEPRAFILM (Genzyme)
see HYALURONIC ACID

- Genzyme is developing a family of surgical products designed to reduce adhesion formation in a wide range of surgical procedures
- these products are made from hyaluronic acid, a biopolymer produced naturally by the body to lubricate and protect tissues
- **Seprafilm:** first of these products to reach the market; it is a bioresorbable membrane, a film that looks like a sheet of waxed paper. It is used to separate and protect tissues damaged by incisions, suturing or cauterisation
- **Sepracoat coating solution:** a liquid formulation of hyaluronic acid used to treat incidental damage to internal tissues as a result of handling and drying due to exposure
- **Sepragel bioresorbable gel:** an investigational product used for surfaces that are inaccessible to Seprafilm during open surgery

SEROTULLE (Leo, distributed by SSL, DT)
see CHLORHEXIDINE, BACTIGRAS

- Chlorhexidine Gauze Dressing BP
- sterile tulle dressing impregnated with White Soft Paraffin BP containing Chlorhexidine Acetate BP 0.5% w/w
- indicated for the prevention of infection in minor wounds

SETOPRIME (SSL, DT)
see NON/LOW ADHERENT DRESSINGS

SILASTIC FOAM
see CAVI-CARE (relaunched in April 1994 by S & N)

SILGEL TOPICAL CREAM (Nagor, DT)
see SILICONE DRESSINGS

- a topical cream of clear, high molecular weight polysiloxane silicone in a 10ml tube

- when applied to the skin it is non-visible, water-repellent and permeable, allowing the skin to breathe in humid conditions
- used for the treatment and control of hypertrophic and keloid scars and selected erythematous conditions
- should be used on clean intact skin surfaces only; do not apply to skin which has not healed or is infected
- applied sparingly once or twice daily
- do not cover on exposed body areas
- excess amounts may stain overlying clothing. To protect clothing wait 15 minutes after massaging and cover lightly with gauze or other material
- between applications wash skin with mild soap solution
- the beneficial effects of silicone cream have been demonstrated on scars and keloid[129] and on grafted skin[130]

SILGEL TOPICAL GEL SHEET (Nagor, DT)
see SILICONE DRESSINGS
- a topical reinforced, durable medical grade silicone sheet (non-sterile) containing no additives
- has an outer surface protected by a flexible white covering
- used for the treatment and control of hypertrophic and keloid scars. Can also be used as a splint lining to relieve friction
- should be used on clean intact skin surfaces only; do not apply to skin which has not healed or is infected
- held in position with gauze, tape, light or compression garments
- firm pressure is not required for therapeutic effect
- should be washed daily with mild soap and water (not detergents)
- available in square, rectangular and shaped sizes

SILICONE DRESSINGS
see CICA-CARE, MEPIFORM, MEPILEX, MEPITEL, N–A ULTRA, SILGEL, SILICONE GEL, SIL–K FILM
- currently it is believed that silicone gel works by promoting hydration of the scar

SILICONE GEL SHEETS (Spenco Medical (UK))
see SILICONE DRESSINGS
- consists of chemically inert, transparent and conformable pure silicone gel
- used to reduce hypertrophic and keloid scarring
- used successfully to flatten scar tissue, increase elasticity and reduce discoloration, regardless of degree, site or age – making the scar cosmetically more acceptable

- Gel sheets may be sterilised in an autoclave; the sheets are re-usable and can be washed in warm water or mild antiseptic solution.

SIL-K FILM (Degania)
see SILICONE DRESSINGS
- soft, durable and transparent silicone sheet less than 1mm thick
- indicated for keloid and hypertrophic scars
- transparent sheet allows users to *see* their scars improving over the two to nine month period advocated for use; can be re-used for many months

SILVER
see ACTISORB SILVER 200, FLAMAZINE, SILVER NITRATE
- silver metal or its salts has antibacterial properties
- long-term use on wounds causes argyria – a general grey discoloration – which is largely a cosmetic problem[59]

SILVER NITRATE
see ANTISEPTICS, SILVER
- formerly used as a 10% solution combined with tannic acid
- 0.5% aqueous solution used for short periods only, then reduce to 0.25%
- use for 2 – 3 days only to avoid toxicity
- has a broad anti-bacterial spectrum (bacteriostatic)
- sometimes used if acetic acid is ineffective against pseudomonas colonisation but has largely been replaced by Flamazine
- painless on application and does not cause local sensitivity
- it stains, making it difficult to delineate between healing and necrotic tissue
- may affect the patient's electrolyte and water balance
- can cause methaemoglobinaemia, argyria and metabolic disturbances
- overgranulation is sometimes treated using 0.25% compresses, or with a silver nitrate stick for more exuberant tissue, and curettage if necessary

SILVER SULFADIAZINE
see FLAMAZINE

SKIN GRAFTS[131]
- different types known as:
  - autographs – taken from patient's own uninjured skin or grown from patient's skin cells into a dressing;
  - allographs – applied as a sheet of bioengineered skin grown from donor cells;
  - xerographs – preserved skin from other animals e.g. pigs

- there is limited evidence that artificial skin used in conjunction with compression bandaging, increases the chance of healing a venous ulcer compared with compression alone

SKIN-PREP (S & N)

see BARRIER FILMS

- contains isopropyl alcohol, butyl ester of PVM/MA copolymer, acetyl tributyl citrate
- available as wipes, aerosol and brush-on form
- protects sensitive skin when used under ostomy appliances, adhesive bandaging, orthopaedic plaster casts
- sting will be experienced if Skin-Prep contacts cut or open wounds
- can reduce erythema caused by trauma from skin tapes[132]

SKIN SUBSTITUTES[69, 133]

see APLIGRAF, BIOBRANE, DERMAGRAFT

- these are tissue engineered products using living cells (fibroblasts, keratinocytes) together with natural or synthetic extracellular matrices as scaffolds which provide mechanical stability and a three-dimensional framework for subsequent tissue infiltration and development
- biodegradable scaffold materials are often used – these are resorbed as new tissue is laid down
- natural scaffolds are derived from human or animal tissues e.g. collagen and hyaluronan
- synthetic scaffolds can be manufactured on a large scale e.g. polyglycolic acid and polylactic acid
- cells consist of three types:
  - *Epidermal:* grafts of cultured epidermal cells with no dermal components e.g. cultured autologous epidermal cells, cultured allogenic epidermal cells, Epicel, LaserSkin. Culture time may be prolonged and there may be difficulties with handling
  - *Dermal:* helps to prevent wound contraction and provides greater mechanical stability e.g. allogenic skin, bovine collagen, Biobrane, Alloderm, Dermagraft, Integra, TransCyte
  - *Combined Dermal/Epidermal:* e.g. composite cultured skin, Apligraf. Care must be taken to apply the dermal layer in contact with the wound bed
- used for burns and more difficult, recalcitrant wounds
- promote wound healing by stimulating the host to produce a variety of cytokines

- the condition of the wound bed will affect product efficacy
- advantages: readily available; do not require painful and invasive procedures; may be used in out-patients
- disadvantages: high cost; potential disease transmission; limited viability (do not survive indefinitely)

SKINTACT (Robinson, DT)
see NON/LOW ADHERENT DRESSINGS
- apertured film on both sides of dressing alleviates worry of dressing being applied incorrectly
- cotton absorbent pad of dressing can cope with low to medium exuding wounds

SODIUM CHLORIDE
see ASKINA JET/SPRAY, IRRICLENS, MESALT, NORMASOL, SALINE STERIPOULES, STERIJET SALINE, STERIPOD SODIUM CHLORIDE, STERZAC SODIUM CHLORIDE
- sterile solutions of 0.9% w/v sodium chloride available in aerosols, sachets and ampoules (Steripods), ideal for topical irrigation and cleansing of wounds
- safe, non-irritant and non-toxic
- has no antiseptic properties but dilutes the concentrations of bacteria in the wound

SOFFBAN NATURAL (S & N, DT)
- 100% viscose fleece
- a sub-compression wadding bandage used as a component of multi-layer compression bandaging

SOFFBAN PLUS (S & N)
- 90% polyester with 10% acrylic fibre containing Triclosan (odour controlling agent)
- synthetic orthopaedic padding which can reduce the risk of unpleasant odours developing under a cast

SOFRA-TULLE (Aventis, DT, POM)
see ANTIBIOTICS
- Framycetin Gauze Dressing BP
- sterile dressing consisting of a cotton leno fabric impregnated with white soft paraffin and lanolin containing 1% w/w framycetin sulphate

- used for infected wounds and has a wide range of antibacterial activity
- should be cut to shape the wound; requires a secondary dressing
- potential cause of hypersensitivity as it contains 10% lanolin and framycetin
- cross-sensitisation may occur with neomycin, kanamycin, etc.
- if used on large body areas, absorption of antibiotic may produce ototoxicity
- not recommended

SOHFAST (Robinson, DT)
- sub-compression wadding bandage

SOLVALINE N (Lohmann, distributed by Vernon-Carus, DT)
see NON/LOW ADHERENT DRESSINGS
- perforated film, medium absorbency dressing with fast wicking action
- finely perforated 100% polyester fabric cover over a 100% cotton inner
- available in sterile and non-sterile dressings

SORBALGON (Hartmann, DT)
see ALGINATE DRESSINGS
- sterile, non-woven dressing of calcium alginate made from marine brown algae
- can be used to cover or lightly fill a wide range of moist wounds, even when infection is present
- **Sorbalgon** is available in two square sizes: 5x5cm and 10x10cm
- **Sorbalgon T** tamponade strips are available as 2g/30cm for deep wounds

SORBSAN (Maersk, DT)
see ALGINATE DRESSINGS
- sterile dressing of Calcium Alginate BPC derived from seaweed harvested off the coast of West Scotland. This seaweed, *Ascophyllum nodosum*, has a higher mannuronic acid level and produces a soft amorphous gel
- available in three forms :
  - **Flat, surgical dressing** – for shallow wet wounds and ulcers
  - **Surgical packing** – 30cm long for large, deep, open wet wounds
  - **Ribbon** 40cm long (plus sterile medical probe) – for smaller, deep, open wet wounds; large, wet wound sinuses and wet wounds in awkward locations, e.g. toes and breasts. The probe can be used to assess the extent of the wound size and shape
- may be applied to a wide range of shallow, heavily to medium exuding lesions, even when infection is present[128]

82

- when in contact with wound secretions containing sodium ions, the insoluble calcium alginate is partially converted to soluble sodium alginate. This forms a hydrophilic gel
- in a clinical comparison of Kaltostat Cavity Dressing and Sorbsan Packing and Ribbon, there was no significant clinical difference in analgesic requirements, mean pain scores or bacterial counts at each dressing change. Nursing staff favoured the handling properties of Sorbsan and its availability in two product sizes[13]

SORBSAN PLUS (Maersk, DT)

see SORBSAN
- consists of three layers :-
  - Sorbsan wound contact layer (cream-coloured)
  - Secondary absorbent viscose pad
  - Upper viscose/polyester layer (blue) – signifies the surface not for wound contact
- can be used without a secondary dressing
- may be applied to a wide range of shallow, heavily to medium exuding wounds, even when infection is present

SORBSAN SA (Maersk)

see SORBSAN. (Sorbsan SA = Sorbsan Self Adhesive)
- an all-in-one dressing consisting of two layers :
  1. Sorbsan wound contact layer bonded centrally to –
  2. Larger waterproof polyurethane foam cover
- may be applied to a wide range of shallow, medium to lightly exuding lesions but not on clinically infected wounds
- changed when a small translucent bubble becomes visible beneath the foam

SPRAY-ON BIODEGRADABLE FIBRES (Electrosols)

- A spray-on extracellular matrix to help wounds heal without scarring has been developed by Electrosols, a biotechnology company in Haslemere[134]
- spray produces a fine web of biodegradable polymer fibres which encourages growth of fibroblasts and a collagen structure
- not yet tested in humans

SPRILON (S & N)

see BARRIER FILMS
- an aerosol containing zinc oxide 12.5% and dimeticone 350, 1.04% (CFC free)

- for prophylaxis and treatment of pressure ulcers, skin maceration due to faeces or urine, or around fistulae and ileostomies
- the flexible film formed on the skin allows normal trans-epidermal water loss
- should not be used on patients allergic to wool fat

SPYROSORB (S & N, DT)
see FOAMS
- sterile, absorbent, vapour-permeable dressing consisting of three layers:
  - Pressure sensitive hydrophilic adhesive
  - Absorbent microporous polyurethane membrane
  - Outer moisture responsive vapour-permeable polyurethane film
- the moisture vapour permeability of the outer layer changes in response to varying levels of exudate production, but remains impermeable to bacteria and water
- used for lightly to medium exuding wounds
- absorbed exudate can be seen through the outer surface and appears as a stain. This is not strike through
- not recommended for use on clinically infected wounds
- should be changed after seven days
- may be cut/overlapped if necessary
- in a randomised study, Spyrosorb provided a more favourable healing response and was easier to remove with no fragmentation than Granuflex E in the treatment of grade 2 and 3 pressure sores in the community[135]
- in a randomised study, Spyrosorb was significantly easier to remove than Granuflex E and was associated with less pain at dressing changes in the treatment of grade 2 and 3 pressure sores in hospitalised patients[136]

STERI-DRAPE (3M)
see VAPOUR-PERMEABLE FILMS
- polymeric film coated with a hypoallergenic adhesive on one side
- specifically designed as a surgical, adhesive incise drape

STERIFIX (Hartmann, DT)
see NON/LOW ADHERENT DRESSINGS
- absorbent, perforated dressing with two adhesive border strips
- used for simple wounds and minor injuries with slight exudation

STERIGEL (SSL, DT)
see HYDROGELS
- used for dry, granulating, necrotic or sloughy wounds

- can absorb residual fluid in an exuding wound; its major mode of action, however, is water donation to facilitate autolytic debridement without causing maceration
- in a randomised trial comparing Sterigel with Intrasite in the debridement of necrotic pressure sores, there were no significant differences in comfort, wound odour, surrounding skin condition or time to debridement[91]
- packed in sealed 15g plastic tubes with snap-off heads

STERIPOD CHLORHEXIDINE (SSL)
see ANTISEPTICS, CHLORHEXIDINE
- sterile solution of chlorhexidine gluconate 0.05% w/v in purified water (20ml)
- used as a topical antimicrobial cleansing solution for the swabbing of wounds and burns

STERIPOD CHLORHEXIDINE AND CETRIMIDE (SSL)
see ANTISEPTICS, CETRIMIDE, CHLORHEXIDINE
- sterile solution of chlorhexidine gluconate 0.015% w/v and cetrimide 0.15% w/v in purified water (20ml)
- used as a topical antimicrobial cleansing solution and for swabbing (but cetrimide is toxic to wound tissues)

STERIPOD SODIUM CHLORIDE (SSL)
see SODIUM CHLORIDE
- sterile solution of sodium chloride 0.9% w/v in purified water (20ml); Steripods are disposable, sealed, blow-moulded, semi-rigid containers made of polyethylene
- Steripods can be poured, used as a dropper or as a syringe to direct the flow of solution; they are an economic alternative to sachets, galley pots, syringes, etc. for wound cleansing

STERZAC SODIUM CHLORIDE (Galen)
see SODIUM CHLORIDE
- sterile sodium chloride 0.9% solution (150ml)

SUCRALFATE
- non-healing venous stasis ulcers may benefit from the angiogenic activity of topical sucralfate[137]

SUDOCREM (Pharmax)
- an antiseptic emollient cream containing zinc oxide, lanolin (hypo-allergenic), benzyl benzoate, benzylcinnamate and benzyl alcohol

- used to treat pressure ulcers, minor burns and surface wounds
- not recommended as there are blander, less-complex products available

SUGAR PASTE[138]
see HONEY

- sugar has been used for centuries in wound care, e.g., honey to debride wounds and for its antibacterial effects
- thin and thick sugar pastes have been developed at Northwick Park Hospital[139]:

	Thin	Thick
Caster sugar (fine granular sucrose)	1200g	1200g
Icing sugar (additive-free, powdered sucrose)	1800g	1800g
Polyethylene glycol 400	1416ml	686ml
Hydrogen peroxide 30%	23.1ml	19ml

- both pastes are chemically stable for at least six months at 4°C
- additive-free icing sugar can be obtained from Tate and Lyle
- both pastes are used to clean up infected, dirty, malodorous wounds
- thin sugar paste can be instilled into wounds with small openings, using a syringe and quill; thick sugar paste can be moulded with a sterile glove and packed into wounds with a large openings
- twice daily packing of wounds is necessary (or more often)
- some patients find sugar paste dressings painful
- sugar paste lowers the pH of wounds to approximately pH5
- sugar may exert its antibacterial effect by competing for the water present in the cells of bacteria
- Northwick Park has many years' experience of the use of Sugar Paste and has found that even the most offensive wounds are usually fully deodorised within three days; in this respect Sugar Paste is the most effective treatment of "smelly" wounds that they have come across
- sugar is readily available and cheap
- sucrose (a disaccharide of glucose and fructose) if absorbed from a wound, is excreted unchanged in urine
- polyethylene glycol 400 can be absorbed from mucous membranes and high blood levels may be nephrotoxic; sugar paste should be used with care in patients with impaired renal function as any absorbed polyethylene glycol is excreted renally
- sugar paste may cause bleeding when granulation tissue is well formed
- no toxic effects were observed with sugar paste which may be preferable to antiseptics for the management of dirty or infected wounds[140]

- water activity and bacterial growth inhibition have been studied for both sucrose and xylose pastes[141]

SUPERSKIN (Medlogic Global, POM)
see BARRIER FILMS
- a non-sterile, solvent-free skin protectant and sealant liquid film containing n-butyl cyanoacrylate
- transparent, waterproof and flexible
- for external use on unbroken skin only to help prevent pressure ulcers and blisters
- can be applied around stomas, wound sites and other areas where skin breakdown is likely to occur e.g. surfaces exposed to friction and shear
- protects skin exposed to irritation from moisture e.g. sweat, urine and digestive juices
- sets in approximately 45 seconds after application
- adheres to skin surface contours as a flexible, bendable sheet; for optimal coverage, use approximately 1 drop per square inch
- effective until it wears off naturally by cracking and flaking away as the skin underneath sloughs; re-application may be necessary in 1–2 days
- for single patient use only – do not use on multiple patients

SUPRASORB (Lohmann Rauscher)
- a new range of moist wound dressings consisting of:
  - **Suprasorb A:** calcium alginate dressing and rope
  - **Suprasorb H:** hydrocolloid dressing (standard, thin, sacrum, border)
  - **Suprasorb M:** polyurethane membrane
  - **Suprasorb F:** polyurethane film
  - **Suprasorb G:** gel wound dressing and amorphous gel
  - **Suprasorb C:** collagen wound dressing
- available in Europe (Sept 2000) but not in the UK

SUREPRESS (ConvaTec, DT))
- an elasticated high compression bandage (extensible), type 3c
- incorporates application aids to ensure correct extension and pressure
- can be handwashed in hot soapy water
- **Surepress Absorbent Padding:** a sub-compression wadding bandage used as a component of multi-layer compression bandaging. Protects vulnerable areas and distributes the graduated compression

SURGICEL (J & J)
see HAEMOSTATICS
- sterile, oxidised cellulose which controls bleeding in 2–3 minutes

SURGIPAD (J & J)
- absorbent pad of absorbent cotton and viscose in sleeve of non-woven viscose fabric
- used for heavily exuding wounds requiring frequent dressing changes

SYSTEM 4 (SSL, DT)
see BANDAGES (FOUR-LAYER)

TAP WATER[142]
- the infection rate in acute traumatic soft tissue wounds cleaned with tap water was less than that for wounds cleaned with sterile saline; sterile saline should be replaced with tap water[143]
- tap water of drinking quality can be used to irrigate open traumatic wounds[144]
- the cleansing of chronic wounds with tap water has not yet been subject to clinical trial

TAPELESS PRODUCTS (Mediplus)
- reusable, non-latex dressing holder range
- absorbable stretchable fabric material
- applicable to a wide range of anatomical areas
- Velcro provides quick, reliable, easy to use fastening and adjustment
- fabric material can be customised by cutting without fraying or unravelling
- washable, reusable material using warm water and air drying
- securely positions the primary dressing
- rapid application and removal
- a 'window' allows quick and easy evaluation of the wound site
- no bulk to limit motion of joints

TEGADERM (3M, DT)
see VAPOUR-PERMEABLE FILMS
- consists of a thin polyurethane layer coated with acrylic adhesive
- its unique frame presentation facilitates self-application without causing wrinkling and self-adherence
- may be left in place for up to 10 days
- **Tegaderm HP** (high permeability) dressing – indicated for wounds where moisture accumulation may be a problem

- **Tegaderm IV** dressings – for dressing catheter sites
- **Tegaderm + Pad** combines the features of Tegaderm dressing with an absorbent pad to form an island dressing

TEGAGEN (3M, DT)
see ALGINATE DRESSINGS – formerly called Tegagel
- a non-woven, polysaccharide dressing consisting of condensed fibres of Calcium Alginate BPC derived from pure, natural Scottish seaweed
- used for variety of medium to heavily exuding wounds
- wet or dry, the dressing maintains its shape and will not easily pull apart
- can be cut or folded
- may be left in place until saturated or for up to seven days
- **Tegagen Cavity Dressing:** 30x2cm rope

TEGAPORE (3M)
see MEMBRANES
- made of chemically inert hypoallergenic polyamide net (no adhesive)
- used as an interface between absorbent dressing and wound
- does not shed particles or fibres
- pores allow the passage of exudate from moist wounds
- virtually non-adherent
- becomes transparent when wet with exudate or saline
- can be left in place for extended periods (up to 14 days on clean, exuding wounds)
- requires a secondary dressing

TEGASORB (3M, DT)
see HYDROCOLLOIDS
- consists of sodium carboxymethylcellulose (CMC) and cross-linked CMC dispersed in a synthetic rubber matrix to give pliability
- border preparation has an outer covering of Tegaderm film extending beyond the hydrocolloid oval – the absorbent mass forms an island in the centre of the film
- used for medium to heavily exuding wounds
- available in bordered oval and non-bordered square shapes

TEGASORB THIN (3M, DT)
see HYDROCOLLOIDS
- consists of sodium carboxymethylcellulose (CMC) and cross-linked CMC dispersed in a synthetic rubber matrix to give pliability

- border preparation has an outer covering of Tegaderm film extending beyond the hydrocolloid oval – the absorbent mass forms an island in the centre of the film
- used for low to medium exuding wounds
- available in bordered oval and non-bordered square shapes

TELFA (Tyco)
see NON/LOW ADHERENT DRESSINGS
- thin layer of absorbent cotton fibres enclosed in a perforated sleeve

TENDERWET (Hartmann)
- a multi-layer wound dressing pad containing a superabsorbent polyacrylate core with irrigating properties as its central component
- used for wound cleansing when wet therapy is needed
- while it is still in its package, the dressing is activated before use with an appropriate volume of Ringer's solution which is then delivered continuously to the wound for up to 24 hours. This actively softens and detaches necrotic tissue. The absorbent core takes up and retains micro-organisms and wound exudate. These two actions simultaneously rinse and cleanse the wound
- upper moisture repellent layer prevents strike through of the dressing
- dressings should be changed once daily
- **Tenderwet 24** delivers set volumes of Ringer's Solution for about 24 hours and therefore should be changed daily. Has a moisture repellent layer beneath the top layer
- **Tenderwet Standard** delivers set volumes of Ringer's Solution for about 12 hours and therefore should be changed twice daily. This does not have an upper moisture repellent layer. Particularly suitable for deep wounds
- both dressings are available in 4 different sizes and shapes (but not yet in the Drug Tariff)

TERRA-CORTRIL (Pfizer)
- hydrocortisone/oxytetracycline ointment
- used widely by plastic surgeons for hypertrophic, oedematous granulating wounds
- commonly believed that steroids have a direct action in decreasing the size and porosity of the granulations which allows the antibiotic access to the fine spaces between the granulation tissue
- should only be used sparingly for a short period

TIELLE (J & J, DT)
see FOAMS
- a particulate-free, synthetic hydropolymer; island dressing consisting of:
  - a waterproof, permeable, polyurethane backing which acts as a barrier to micro-organisms
  - skin-friendly adhesive
  - non-woven wicking layer (fluid transport)
  - highly absorbent hydropolymer central island which expands as exudate is taken up
- a hydropolymer is a non-particulate polymer or mixture of polymers, the polymers being hydrophilic and interactive with aqueous fluids
- does not liquefy or breakdown and therefore leaves no particulate matter in the wound
- in a randomised controlled clinical study comparing Tielle with Granuflex, Tielle was better in preventing leakage and reducing odour, but there were no differences in healing rates of patients with leg ulcers or pressure ulcers[62]
- provides a moist healing environment which allows granulation to proceed under optimum conditions
- used for low to medium exuding wounds
- should not be used on clinically infected wounds without medical supervision
- does not require a secondary dressing
- suitable for use under compression bandaging
- may be left *in situ* for up to 7 days depending on exudate levels
- adhesive border and sacral dressing also available in DT

TIELLE LITE (J & J, DT)
see FOAMS AND TIELLE
- a sterile, polyurethane, foam, film dressing
- used for dry to low exuding wounds
- available as square and rectangular dressings with borders

TIELLE PLUS (J & J, DT)
see FOAMS AND TIELLE
- a sterile, polyurethane foam, film dressing indicated for medium to heavily exuding wounds
- available as square and rectangular dressings with adhesive borders
- **Tielle Plus Borderless:** square dressings without adhesive border

TISEPT (SSL)
see CHLORHEXIDINE, CETRIMIDE
- contains chlorhexidine gluconate (0.015%) and cetrimide (0.15%) in a clear yellow aqueous solution
- not recommended for wound care because of cetrimide content

TOPIGEL (Inamed)
- a soft, slightly adhesive, semi-occlusive polyester fabric reinforced gel sheet
- used to treat keloid and hypertrophic scarring

TRENTAL (Borg, POM)
see PENTOXIFYLLINE

TRICOTEX (S & N, DT)
see NON/LOW ADHERENT DRESSINGS
- a sterile, knitted viscose primary dressing

TULLE (MEDICATED) DRESSINGS
see BACTIGRAS, FUCIDIN INTERTULLE, INADINE, M AND M, POVIDERM, SEROTULLE, SOFRA-TULLE
- used for infected, superficial wounds
- on the basis of evidence available to date, it appears that chlorhexidine tulle gras is the superior product[145]

TULLE (NON-MEDICATED) DRESSINGS
see ATRAUMAN, PARAFFIN GAUZE / TULLE GRAS (NON-MEDICATED)

ULTEC (Kendall)
see HYDROCOLLOIDS
- unavailable in the UK

ULTRA FOUR (Robinson Healthcare, DT)
see BANDAGES (FOUR-LAYER)

UNISEPT (SSL)
see CHLORHEXIDINE
- contains chlorhexidine gluconate (0.05% w/v) in a clear, pink aqueous solution
- available in 25ml and 100ml sterile sachets
- used as a general antiseptic for swabbing wounds and burns

UNITULLE (Aventis, DT)

see PARAFFIN GAUZE / TULLE GRAS

- a "light loaded" sterile product containing 90 to 130g of paraffin base per square metre of cloth
- is contra-indicated where there is known allergy to lanolin

VACUUM-ASSISTED CLOSURE (VAC) THERAPY (KCI Medical)

- the VAC unit applies negative pressure to a specialised dressing positioned in the wound cavity or over a flap or graft. Excess fluid is collected in a disposable canister
- helps to reduce oedema, increase blood supply and decrease bacterial colonisation
- the therapy has proven to be effective with cardiothoracic surgical wounds[146], pressure ulcers, chronic wounds and grafts

VAPOUR-PERMEABLE FILMS

see ARGLAES, ASKINA DERM, BIOCLUSIVE, CUTIFILM, DERMAFILM, ENSURE-IT, EPIVIEW, HYDROFILM, IOBAN-II, MEFILM, OPRAFLEX, OPSITE FLEXI-GRID, POLYSKIN II, (POLYVINYLCHLORIDE), SUPRASORB F, TEGADERM

- sterile, thin, conformable, vapour-permeable, hypoallergenic adhesive-coated films
- only considered suitable for relatively shallow wounds, e.g., dermabrasion, burns and donor sites. Also used prophylactically to prevent pressure ulcers, as retention dressings, e.g., for cannulas and in theatres for operative surgery (as sterile drapes)
- probably the single most important feature of films is their ability to permit the passage of water vapour from beneath the film to the external environment[147]
- the skin around the wound needs to be clean and dry prior to application of the film
- are variably transparent, depending on the product enabling monitoring of skin and wound
- have many of the characteristics of an ideal dressing (*see* appendix) except:
  - excessive exudate may accumulate under the dressing. This is often aspirated using a sterile syringe – the puncture hole being covered with a small piece of the film. However, it is better practice to remove the film and apply a new dressing. This prevents infecting the wound and eliminates needle-stick injuries;
  - the film may cling to itself during application and may need considerable skill to apply e.g. two pairs of hands;

- may be some adhesive trauma on removal, especially on inflamed, fragile skin;
  - they cool the surface of the wound
- the properties of six semi-permeable film dressings have been compared[148]
- a meta-analysis shows that there is a significantly increased risk of catheter-tip infection with the use of transparent dressings compared with gauze dressings when used with either central or peripheral catheters[149]

VARIDASE (Wyeth, POM)[150]

- sterile vial of dry powder containing two enzymes, streptokinase and streptodornase, which is stored in the refrigerator (2–8°C.)
- **Varidase Topical Combi-Pack** includes the present vial of Varidase powder, a 20ml flip-top vial of sterile normal saline (diluent), a sterile transfer needle and full instructions on the method of reconstitution
- needs to be reconstituted with 20ml sterile sodium chloride 0.9% w/v solution (stable for up to 24 hours stored in a refrigerator at 2–8 °C). Do not shake the vial vigorously when reconstituting otherwise the enzymes will be denatured
- used for cleansing of necrotic and infected wounds and suppurative surface lesions
- needs to be applied once or twice a day and may be covered by a film dressing
- allergic reactions may occur infrequently
- streptokinase degrades fibrin and fibrinogen; streptodornase liquefies and facilitates the removal of DNA derived from cell nuclei. This facilitates cleansing and desloughing of the wound
- as Varidase does not contain a preservative, multi-dose use is not recommended
- can be injected by experienced staff under dry scabs or applied on the surfaces of scabs which have been cross-hatched with a sterile scalpel
- in a randomised, double-blind, controlled trial, a comparison was made of the relative efficacy of using Varidase in KY Jelly or KY Jelly alone. The results suggest that KY Jelly may be a cost effective alternative to the use of Varidase in KY Jelly[95]
- patients treated with topical Varidase all showed an increase in antistreptokinase titres. It would therefore seem prudent to restrict the use of topical streptokinase to patients not at risk of myocardial infarction[151]
- topical streptokinase causes a significant humoral response by one month, which then declines. To ensure thrombolytic efficacy, therefore, it may be preferable to avoid intravenous streptokinase in patients who have been treated with topical streptokinase in the preceding six months[152]

VARIHESIVE (ConvaTec)
see HYDROCOLLOIDS
- wafers containing gelatin 20%, pectin 20%, polyisobutylene 40%, sodium carboxymethylcellulose 20%
- superseded by Granuflex for wound care

VELBAND (J & J)
sub-compression absorbent wadding bandage

VIDENE (Adams)
see POVIDONE-IODINE
- 10% antiseptic solution for pre-operative skin disinfection and general antisepsis

VIGILON (Bard, distributed by SSL)
see HYDROGELS
- a colloidal suspension of radiation cross-linked polyethylene oxide (4%) and water (96%) on a polyethylene mesh support to provide strength
- mainly used for burns and superficial pressure ulcers
- feels wet and cold on touch but is neither
- both sides of the dressing are backed with an inert polyethylene film that controls water vapour transmission
- if a totally breathable dressing is required both films are removed
- for occlusive use, one film is removed and the uncovered face placed on the wound
- thinner than Geliperm and therefore more difficult to apply
- on average needs changing every three days. Heavily exuding wounds may require to be changed daily
- the results of a laboratory study suggest that Vigilon (and Geliperm) are likely to be ideally suited only to wounds that exude at a rate which is compatible with the fluid handling properties of the dressings[61]

YOGHURT
- made from milk which has been heat-treated and then inoculated with harmless bacteria, e .g. *Streptococcus thermophilus, Lactobacillus bulgaricus* or *Lactobacillus acidophilus*
- after the bacteria have multiplied, the mixture is chilled (2 weeks' expiry) or pasteurised (3 months' expiry)
- wound healing folk-lore describes the use of yoghurt but scientific proof is required

- can be used twice daily for three days, then daily
- soothing but messy

ZINC

- a systematic literature review has shown that oral zinc sulphate does not appear to aid healing of leg ulcers, although it might be beneficial in those with venous leg ulcers and a low serum zinc. Further research is needed to verify this and if so to ascertain the serum zinc concentration below which treatment with zinc is beneficial, and to ascertain the optimum treatment regimen[153]

ZINC SULPHATE LOTION (Lotio Rubra)

- Zinc sulphate 1%, with amaranth, in water
- apply undiluted as a wet dressing

ZIPZOC (S & N)

- a sterile rayon stocking impregnated with 20% zinc oxide ointment and no preservatives
- used for treatment of chronic leg ulcers and chronic venous insufficiency
- applied from the base of the toes to below the knee
- can be used as the primary contact layer and under compression bandaging
- should be changed at least weekly
- not as absorbent as paste bandages – exudate passes through stocking into a secondary pad
- one size comfortably fits legs 14 to 60cm in circumference
- to protect clothes from Zipzoc, a suitable outer bandage should be worn
- a licensed medicine and is available on NHS prescription, however it is not a medical device and therefore will not appear under section IXA of the DT

DISCONTINUED PRODUCTS

Algistat
Askina Biofilm S
Bard Absorption Dressing
Clorhexitulle
Colgen
Corethium 1 and 2
Debrisan Absorbent Pad
Dermalex
Dermasorb Spiral
Fibracol
Geliperm Dry Sheets
Granuflex hydrocolloid compression
    bandage
Histoacryl
Interface V–C
Jelonet (10 pieces)
Kaltocarb
Kaltoclude
Kaltostat Fortex

Lyofoam X
Malatex
Omiband
Ominatal
Opragel
Perfron
Pharmaclusive
Polybactrim
Rikospray
Spenco 2nd Skin
Sterijet Saline
Surfasoft
Tegaderm Plus
Transite
Tribiotic
Variclene
Vigilon (non-sterile)
Vivoderm

WOUND MANAGEMENT PRODUCTS IN THE DRUG TARIFF[154]

In the early 1980s, very few dressings were available apart from traditional dressings and paste bandages. The first representatives of modern wound management products became available in hospitals during the mid 1980s but did not become available in primary care until 1988 when Inadine, Granuflex, Kaltostat and Sorbsan were added to the Drug Tariff. Up until 1995, further products were cautiously added following careful evaluation. Many primary care practitioners e.g. nurses and wound care groups, complained about the limited choice in the Drug Tariff.

From 1996, however, this considered approach appears to have been abandoned as an avalanche of new products have been added both to the Drug Tariff and to the list of preparations which can be prescribed by nurses, Part XVIIB of the Drug Tariff. There is limited information available about these products e.g. evidence of effectiveness of individual products or of comparative effectiveness. In fact, when added to the Drug Tariff, it is often very difficult to find out basic details such as the name of the manufacturer of the product!

Year	Number of products added to the Drug Tariff
1988	4
1989	1
1990	4
1991	4
1992	2
1993	5
1994	4
1995	5
1996	12
1997	15
1998	26
1999	67
2000	43 (until October 2000)

MANAGEMENT OF WOUNDS/WOUND TYPES[155, 156]

DISCOLOURED, UNBROKEN SKIN
- Dry skin : simple bland ointments e.g. yellow/white soft paraffin
- Skin conditions associated with wounds: paste bandages
- Skin subject to pressure or trauma: foam dressings; low-adherent dressings; non-medicated tulles; vapour-permeable films

FLAT, DRY WOUNDS
- Low-adherent dressings; vapour-permeable films; membranes

EPITHELIALISING WOUNDS
- dressing choice depends on level of exudate
- Vapour-permeable films; membranes; paraffin tulle
- Hydrocolloids; Hydrogels
- Alginates; foams
- Low-adherent dressings

FLAT, MOIST WOUNDS
- Low-adherent dressings; non-medicated tulles; vapour-permeable films;
- Membranes; hydrocolloids; hydrogels; foams; alginates

GRANULATING WOUNDS
- dressing choice depends on level of exudate and depth of wound
- Hydrocolloids; alginates; foams; hydrogels

EXUDING WOUNDS[157]
1. Light-medium exudate
   - Foams
   - Alginates: Curasorb, Sorbsan SA
   - Hydrocolloids: transparent dressings; thin dressings; Combiderm
   - Hydrogel: wet Geliperm
   - Hydroactives: Cutinova Thin
2. Medium – heavy exudate
   - Alginates
   - Hydrocolloids: Aquacel, Hydrocoll
   - Foams: Tielle Plus
   - Hydroactives: Cutinova Foam, Cutinova Hydro
   - Drawtex

3. Heavy exudate
   - Algosteril, Allevyn; Kaltogel, Lyofoam Extra, Mesalt, Seasorb, Sorbsan Plus

CAVITY WOUNDS[158, 159]

– Foams:	Allevyn Cavity Wound Dressing; Cavi-Care
– Alginate:	rope, ribbon, cavity dressings
– Hydroactives:	Cutinova Cavity
– Hydrogels:	gel products;
– Hydrocolloids:	pastes/gels
– Sugar pastes:	thin and thick

- Iodoflex
- Iodosorb ointment $\Big\}$ infected cavities

SLOUGHY WOUNDS[160, 161, 162]

1. Modern products will remove slough and absorb exudate:
   - Hydrogels e.g. gel products, Intrasite Conformable
   - Hydrocolloids e.g. paste/gels
   - Alginates
   - Sugar pastes (thick and thin)
   - Sodium chloride 0.9% w/v irrigation
2. Mechanical debridement
   - scalpel (with or without local/general anaesthetic)
   - wet-to-dry saline-soaked gauze
3. Biosurgical debridement using larvae e.g. Larv E
4. Enzymatic debridement e.g. Varidase
5. Miscellaneous: whirlpool, hydrotherapy, high pressure irrigation

INFECTED WOUNDS

- general infection control measures e.g. hand washing
- Systemic antibiotics – depending on local/systemic signs of infection
- Antibacterials e.g. Flamazine
- Antiseptics e.g. restrict to chlorhexidine and povidone-iodine products

MALODOROUS WOUNDS

- reduce levels of bacterial colonisation
- Activated charcoal dressings
- Sugar paste (thick and thin)
- Metronidazole Gels – use judiciously e.g. for fungating, malodorous tumours only

NECROTIC WOUNDS (e.g. black heel)

- Hydrocolloids
- Hydrogels
- Varidase and/or hydrogels
- mechanical/surgical debridement

MALIGNANT/FUNGATING WOUNDS

- control bleeding
- assess pain and analgesia requirements
- treat or mask odour
- debride wound
- reduce volume of exudate
- reduce inflammation e.g. by removing sensitising agents
- care for surrounding skin
- improve cosmetic appearance e.g. reduce tumour bulk; avoid bulky dressings
- enable patient to cope with altered body image

OEDEMATOUS WOUNDS

- Compression bandages; exercise; elevation of leg

OVER/HYPERGRANULATION TISSUE

- occurs in many types of wounds when the inflammatory phase of healing is prolonged unnecessarily
- ideally any treatment should not further exacerbate the inflammatory reaction and should be non-traumatic
- there is no consensus as to the correct treatment but the most frequently used methods are[163]:
  - change from an occlusive to a non-occlusive dressing such as Lyofoam[164]
  - application of light pressure to the wound bed by the addition of supplementary padding
  - short-term application of a low dose of corticosteroid e.g. Terracortril (tetracycline and hydrocortisone ointment) or Daktacort (miconazole and hydrocortisone cream) – not ideal
  - removal using a caustic substance such as silver nitrate sticks/compresses – not ideal
  - allowing the hypergranulation to resolve itself without treatment
- other less ideal treatments are:
  - currettage; cautery
  - phenol; polysporin

CARE OF SKIN SURROUNDING WOUNDS
- Paste bandages

PARTICULAR WOUNDS
- A precise diagnosis is required:

1. Venous ulcers
   - Compression bandages; elevation; exercise
   - Paste bandages – to treat skin conditions
2. Arterial ulcers
   - Paste bandages to treat skin conditions; exercise
   - Compression bandages are contraindicated
3. Venous/arterial ulcers
   - As for arterial ulcers except that light compression may be indicated
4. Pressure ulcers[165, 166]
   - Relief of pressure
   - the evidence of the effects of dressings is poor[167]
5. Burns and scalds
   - Cold running water (10–15 minutes)
   - Non-medicated paraffin tulles; Flamazine
   - HF-Antidote Gel for hydrofluoric acid burns
6. Diabetic ulcers[168, 169]
   There is evidence of effectiveness of the following for prevention:
   - identification of those at high risk; referral to foot care clinics which offer education, podiatry and footwear
   - therapeutic shoes with custom-moulded insoles
   The following treatments may be beneficial but further trials are required:
   - total contact casting
   - Growth factors
   - G-CSF for patients with severe infections
   - 2% ketanserin ointment
   - Iamin ointment
   - debridement with cadexomer iodine
   - Dermagraft
7. Recalcitrant wounds
   - Growth factors
   - Skin substitutes e.g. Apligraf, Biobrane, Dermagraft
   - Hyalofill

CHARACTERISTICS OF IDEAL DRESSINGS[170]

1. Provide the optimum environment for wound healing – a moist environment–at the wound/dressing interface
2. Allow gaseous exchange of oxygen, carbon dioxide and water vapour
3. Provide thermal insulation – wound healing is temperature dependent
4. Impermeable to micro-organisms (in both directions)
5. Free from particulate contaminants
6. Non-adherent (many products are described as non-adherent but are low-adherent)
7. Safe to use (non-toxic, non-sensitising, non-allergenic)
8. Acceptable to the patient
9. High absorption characteristics (for exuding wounds)
10. Cost effective
11. Carrier for medicaments, e.g. antiseptics
12. Capable of standardisation and evaluation
13. Allow monitoring of the wound (transparent)
14. Provide mechanical protection
15. Non-inflammable
16. Sterilisable
17. Conformable and mouldable (especially over sacrum, heels and elbows)
18. Available (hospital and community) in a suitable range of forms and sizes
19. Require infrequent changing. Products should be left in place for as long as possible – "A bad cook always opens the oven door".

WOUND CARE GROUPS

British Lymphology Society, BLS Administrative Centre, PO Box 1059, Caterham, Surrey CR3 6ZU. Tel: 01883 330253

British Vascular Foundation. Griffin House, West Street, Woking, Surrey GU21 1EB

Community and District Nursing Association. Thames Valley University, 8 University House, Ealing Green, London W5 5ED. Tel: 0208 2312776

European Pressure Ulcer Advisory Panel. Wound Healing Unit, Department of Dermatology, Churchill Hospital, Old Road, Headington, Oxford OX3 7LJ. Fax: 01865 228233. www.epuap.com

European Tissue Repair Society. Aims to promote knowledge and improve contacts to those interested in the healing or related reactions of any organ. Secretariat: Department of Pathology, University of Geneva, 1 rue Michel Servet, 1211 Geneva 4, Switzerland. Tel: 0041 22 229 377. www.leahcim.demon.co.uk/etrs.htm

European Wound Management Association. Promotes advancement of education and research into native epidemiology, pathology, diagnosis, prevention and management of wounds of all aetiologies. Holds conferences and provides grants. PO Box 864, London SE1 8TT. Tel: 0207 848 3496. www.leahcim.demon.co.uk/ewma.htm or www.ewma.com

The Leg Ulcer Forum. CRICP, Wolfson Institute of Health Sciences, 32–38 Uxbridge Road, London W5 2BS. Tel: 0208 280 5020

Tissue Viability Society. Registered charity bringing together the multi-disciplinary skills of health care professionals in order to raise standards of good practice in the prevention and treatment of pressure sores, leg ulcers and chronic wounds. Glanville Centre, Salisbury District Hospital, Salisbury, Wilts SP2 8BJ. Tel: 01722 336262 Ext: 4057. www.tvs.org.uk/

The Venous Forum, Royal Society of Medicine, 1 Wimpole Street, London W1M 8AE. Tel: 0207 408 2119

104

Wound Care Society. A charitable, non-profit based organisation whose main role is the provision of high quality wound care education. PO Box 170, Hartford, Huntingdon PE29 1PL. Tel/Fax: 01480 434401. www.woundcaresociety.org/

JOURNALS

Advances in Skin & Wound Care. A scholarly, peer-reviewed, multidisciplinary journal (formerly *Advances in Wound Care*) features original research, comprehensive clinical reviews, and articles addressing practical management of skin and wound care patients. www.woundcarenet.com/advances.htm

Advances in Wound Care (formerly *Decubitus*). (Springhouse Corporation, USA). Published bi-monthly

Journal of Tissue Viability (Tissue Viability Society, Salisbury). Published quarterly

Journal of Wound Care (emap Healthcare London). Published monthly

Journal of WOCN (Wound, Ostomy and Continence Nursing). (Mosby, USA) An authoritative resource devoted to the nursing care and management of patients with abdominal stomas, wounds, pressure ulcers, fistulas, vascular ulcers and incontinence www1.mosby.com

Nursing Journal of the Tissue Viability Society. Supplement in *Nursing Standard* (RCN Publishing Company). Published quarterly

Ostomy/Wound Management. Journal containing information on the care of patients with ostomies, chronic wounds, incontinence, and related skin and nutritional concerns www.medexpo.co

Tissue Viability Supplement Supplement to *British Journal of Nursing* (Mark Allen Publishing, London). Published quarterly www.internurse.com

Wounds (Health Management Publications, USA). Published bi-monthly.

Wound Repair and Regeneration. The official publication of The Wound Healing Society, the European Tissue Repair Society, the Japanese Society for Wound Healing and the Australian Wound Management Association. Published six times a year. Contains original scientific and/or clinical papers on the broadly defined topics of wound healing and tissue regeneration. wizard.pharm.wayne.edu/wrr/WRR.HTM

World Wide Wounds. Surgical Materials Testing Laboratory's electronic journal www.smtl.co.uk/World-Wide-Wounds/index.html

NURSE PRESCRIBERS' FORMULARY 1999–2001 (NPF)

The second edition of the NPF has been published. It succeeds an earlier edition and two earlier pilot editions prepared for the nurse prescribing demonstration scheme. Subsequent editions will be published biennially. Information is set out as in the BNF and incorporates BNF 38 (Sept 1999). The NPF contains an extensive range of wound management dressings and related products including the following which may be prescribed by nurses on forms FP10(CN) and FP10(PN) (form GP10(N) in Scotland, form HS21(N) in Northern Ireland) for NHS patients:

- Cotton Crepe Bandage
- Hospicrepe 239
- Cotton Stretch Bandage BP 1988
- Multi-layer Compression Bandaging
- Short Stretch Compression Bandage
- Sub-compression Wadding Bandage
- Wound Management Cavity Dressings

Chlorhexidine Gauze Dressing BP, Framycetin Gauze Dressing BP and Sodium Fusidate Gauze Dressing BP are not on the Nurse Prescribers' List.

A *Prescribing Nurse Bulletin* on dressings is available from the National Prescribing Centre website[171]. www.npc.co.uk

ADDITIONAL READING

1. Pressure ulcer treatment guidelines. European Pressure Ulcer Advisory Panel (www.epuap.com)
2. Pressure ulcer prevention guidelines. European Pressure Ulcer Advisory Panel (www.epuap.com)
3. Cutting KF. Wounds and infection. The Wound Care Society. Educational leaflet, August 1998; **5** (2)
4. Vowden K. Vowden P. Leg ulcer assessment. The Wound Care Society. Educational leaflet, November 1998; **5** (3)
5. Bennett G. Graduated compression hosiery. The Wound Care Society. Educational leaflet, May 1999; **6** (1)
6. Hallett A. Hampton S. Wound dressings. The Wound Care Society. Educational leaflet, Feb 1999; **6** (1)
7. Newton H. Eczema aetiology and management. The Wound Care Society. Educational leaflet, Sept 1999; **6** (3)
8. Hollinworth H. Pain and wound care. The Wound Care Society. Educational leaflet, May 2000; **7** (2)
9. Culley F. Legal and professional issues in tissue viability revisited. The Wound Care Society. Educational leaflet, February 2000; **7** (1)
10. Thomas S, Toyick N, Fisher B. Graduated external compression and the prevention of deep vein thrombosis. Surgical Materials Testing Laboratory, Bridgend 2000
11. Morgan DA. Setting up wound care guidelines: Avoiding the pitfalls. *J Tissue Viability* 1998; **8**(3): 5–8
12. Gallenkemper G, Rabe E, Bauer R. Contact sensitisation in chronic venous insufficiency: modern wound dressings. *Contact Dermatitis* 1998; **38:** 274–278
13. Thomas S. The importance of secondary dressings in wound care. *J Wound Care* 1998; **7**(4): 189–192
14. Renton EJ. Pharmacological treatments for venous leg ulcers. *J Wound Care* 1999; **8**(4): 195–197
15. The care of patients with chronic leg ulcer, National clinical guideline, Scottish Intercollegiate Guidelines Network, publication 26, July 1998
16. Briggs M, Nelson EA. Topical agents or dressings for pain in venous leg ulcers (Cochrane Review). In: Cochrane Library, Issue 3, 2000. Oxford: Update Software

OTHER WEB SITES

American Academy of Wound Management. Certifying board in the USA for healthcare professionals involved in wound care
members.aol.com/woundnet/

Association for the Advancement of Wound Care. World-wide collaboration to advance the cause of wound care (based in the USA)
www.medexpo.com/hmp/aawc.html

Biosurgical Research Unit (SMTL, Bridgend). Specialises in breeding maggots for sale and researching their use in wound care
www.smtl.co.uk/WMPRC/BioSurgery/index.html

Cochrane Wounds Group. Abstracts of Cochrane Reviews, The Cochrane Library Issue 3, 2000. Access to full text of reviews and protocols
www.update-software.com/cochrane/cochrane-frame.html

Industry sites
Information on manufacturers of dressings and medical disposables
www.smtl.co.uk/Manufacturers/index.html

Pressure Sore Web Forum. An on-line discussion forum
www.medicaledu.com/pressure_sore_forum/

Surgical Materials Testing Laboratory (Bridgend). Home page of SMTL, with links to *World Wide Wounds* and all related web sites. www.smtl.co.uk/

SMTL Discussion Forum for wound management related issues
www.smtl.co.uk/cgi-bin/HyperNews/get.cgi/wounds.html

Venous Stasis Ulcer Web Forum. An on-line discussion forum
www.medicaledu.com/venous_stasis_forum/

Wound Care Information Network. www.medicaledu.com/

Wound Care Web Forum. medicaledu.com/wound_care_forum/

Wound Healing Society. Non-profit, international organisation for those interested in the field of wound healing. www.woundhealsoc.org

Wound Management Practice Resource Centre. An independent site with financial assistance from the Welsh Value for Money Unit. Source of information on Biosurgery (maggots and leeches), dressings (data cards), medical devices and the treatment of many different kinds of wounds. Also an electronic wound journal, *World Wide Wounds*, which was launched on July 14th 1997. Site is maintained by the Surgical Materials Testing Laboratory, Bridgend. www.smtl.co.uk/

Wound Ostomy Continence Nursing Society. A professional nursing society which promotes educational, clinical, and research opportunities, to advance the practice and guide the delivery of expert health care to individuals with wounds, ostomies and incontinence. www.wocn.org/

HELPLINES (freephones)

3M Health Care:	0800 616066	
B Braun:	0800 163007 (UK);	1800 409538 (Ireland)
CliniMed:	0800 585125	
Coloplast:	0800 220622 (UK);	1800 409502 (Ireland)
ConvaTec:	0800 289738 (UK);	1800 721721 (Ireland)
J&J:	0800 839154	
Mölnlycke:	0800 7311876	
S & N:	0800 590173	

OTHER HELPLINES

Robinson:	01246 505450
Hartmann:	01706 363320
Huntleigh:	0345 585688 (Lo-call)

FINAL COMMENT

There is little evidence to indicate which dressings or topical agents are the most effective in the treatment of chronic wounds. There is good evidence that compression is useful for the treatment of venous leg ulcers. In the treatment of venous ulcers, low adherent dressings are as effective as hydrocolloid dressings beneath compression bandaging. Hydrocolloid dressings are better than wet-to-dry dressings for the treatment of pressure sores[172]. The effects of occlusive and non occlusive dressings compared with simple dressings have not yet been adequately evaluated in randomised controlled trials[173].

UPDATES TO FORMULARY

The Formulary of Wound Management Products will be regularly updated on the Publishers' website as new products are launched and further technical information becomes available:
www.euromed.uk.com/formulary.htm

REFERENCES

1. Phillips I, Lobo AZ, Fernandes R, Gundara LS. Acetic acid in the treatment of superficial wounds infected by *Pseudomonas aeruginosa*. *Lancet* 1968; **1:** 11–13
2. Milner SM. Acetic acid to treat *Pseudomonas aeruginosa* in superficial wounds and burns. *Lancet* 1992; **340:** 61 (letter)
3. Application of alcohol. *J Wound Care* 1992; **1**(2):53
4. Morgan DA. Alginate dressings. Part 1: Historical Aspects. *J Tissue Viability* 1997; **7**(1): 4–9
5. Morgan DA. Alginate dressings. Part 2: Product Guide. *J Tissue Viability* 1997; **7**(1): 9–14.
6. Thomas S, Loveless P. Observations on the fluid handling properties of alginate dressings. *Pharm J* 1992; **248:** 850–851
7. Johnson BJ, Simpson C. A laboratory comparison of alginate dressings. *Pharm J* 1993. **251:** 46
8. Agren MS. Four alginate dressings in the treatment of partial thickness wounds: a comparative experimental study. *Br J Plastic Surgery* 1996; **49**(2): 129–134.
9. Berry DP, Bale S, Harding KG. Dressings for treating cavity wounds. *J Wound Care* 1996; **5**(1): 10–13
10. Sayag J, Meaume S, Bohbot S. Healing properties of calcium alginate dressings. *J Wound Care* 1996; **5**(8): 357–362
11. Bale S, Squires D, Varnon T, Walker A, Benbow M, Harding KG. A comparison of two dressings in pressure sore management. *J Wound Care* 1997; **6**(10): 463–466.
12. Butterworth RJ, *et al.* Comparing Allevyn Cavity Wound Dressings and Silastic Foam. *J Wound Care* 1992 ; **1**(1) : 10–13.
13. Williams P *et al.* A comparison of two alginate dressings in the management of acute wound cavities. In: Proceedings of the 4th European Conference on Advances in Wound Management, eds Cherry GW, Leaper DJ, Lawrence JC, Milward P, 1995; 55–56. London, Macmillan Magazines.
14. Lineaweaver W, Howard R, Soucy D *et al.* Topical Antimicrobial toxicity. *Arch Surg* 1985; **120:** 267–270
15. Infection control in general practice Part 5: topical drugs. Supplement to *MIMS Magazine* 1993; 29 June: 1–8
16. Morison M. Wound Cleansing—Which Solution? *Nursing Standard* 1990; **4**(52): 4–6
17. Leaper DJ, Simpson RA. The effect of antiseptics and topical antimicrobials on wound healing. *J Antimicrob Chemother* 1986; **17:** 135–137
18. Morgan DA. Is there still a role for antiseptics? *J Tissue Viability* 1993; **3**(3): 80–84
19. Lawrence JC, Harding KG, Moore DJ. The use of antiseptics in wound care. *J Wound Care* 1996; **5**(1): 44–47
20. Mimoz O, Karim A, Mercat A *et al.* Chlorhexidine compared with povidone-iodine as skin preparation before blood culture. *Ann Intern Med.* 1999; **131:** 834–837
21. Armstrong SH, Ruckley CV. Use of a fibrous dressing in exuding leg ulcers. J *Wound Care* 1997; **6**(7): 322–324
22. Thomas S, Hay NP. *In vitro* investigations of a new hydrogel dressing. *J Wound Care* 1996; **5**(3): 130–131
23. Layton AM, Ibbotson SH, Davies JA, Goodfield MJD.. Randomised trial of oral aspirin for chronic venous leg ulcers. *Lancet* 1994; **344:** 164–165
24. Ibbotson SH *et al.* The effect of aspirin on haemostatic activity in the treatment of chronic venous leg ulceration. *Br J Dermatol* 1995; **132:** 422–426
25. Ruckley CV, Prescott RJ. Treatment of chronic leg ulcers. *Lancet 1994; 344:* 1512–1513
26. Thomas S *et al.* Improvements in medicated tulle dressings. *J Hosp Infect* 1983; **4:** 391–398
27. Stockport JC, Groarke L, Ellison DA, McCollum C. Single-layer and multilayer bandaging in the treatment of venous leg ulcers. *J Wound Care* 1997; **6**(10): 485–488
28. Morrell CJ, Walters SJ, Dixon S *et al.* Cost effectiveness of community leg ulcer clinics: randomised controlled trial. *Br Med J* 1998; **316:** 1487–1491

29. Cullum N, Nelson EA, Fletcher AW, Sheldon TA, Song F, Fletcher AW. Compression for venous leg ulcers (Cochrane Review). In: *Cochrane Library*, Issue 3, 2000. Oxford: Update Software
30. *Effective Health Care Bulletin* August 1997, Volume 3, Number 4
31. Carr L, Phillips Z, Posnett J. Comparative cost-effectiveness of four layer bandaging in the treatment of venous leg ulceration. *J Wound Care* 1999; **8:** 243–248
32. Moffatt CJ, Dickson D. The Charing Cross high compression four-layer bandage system. *J Wound Care* 1993; **2**(2): 91–94
33. Lawrence JC. A first-aid preparation for burns and scalds. *J Wound Care* 1996; **5**(6): 262–264
34. Dunn RJ. Practical application of a first-aid treatment for burns and scalds. *J Wound Care* 1996; **5**(6): 265–266
35. Rotheli-Simmen B, Martinelli E, Muhlebach S. Formulation of a stable calcium gluconate gel for topical treatment of hydrofluoric acid burns. *EHP* 1996; **2**(4): 176–180
36. Wood RAB. Foam elastomer dressing in the management of open granulating wounds: experience with 280 patients. *Br J Surg* 1977; **64:** 554–557
37. Cooper R, Bale S, Harding JG. An improved cleaning regime for a modified foam cavity dressing. *J Wound Care* 1995; **4**(1): 13–16
38. Thomas S, Hay N.P, Wound Cleansing. *Pharm J* 1985; **235:** 206 (letter)
39. McLure AR, Gordon J. *In vitro* evaluation of povidone-iodine and chlorhexidine against methicillin-resistant *Staphylococcus aureus*. *J Hosp Infect* 1992; **21:** 291–299
40. Cheung J, O'Leary JJ. Allergic reaction to chlorhexidine in an anaesthetised patient. *Anaesth Intensive Care* 1985; **13:** 429–430
41. Evans RJ. Acute anaphylaxis due to topical chlorhexidine acetate. *Br Med J* 1992; **304:** 686 (letter)
42. Morgan DA. Wound Care: Chlorinated Solutions—E(useful) or (e)useless. *Pharm J* 1989; **243:** 219–220
43. Morgan DA. Chlorinated Solutions—An Update. *J Tissue Viability* 1991; **1**(2): 31–33
44. Moore D. Hypochlorites: a review of the evidence. *J Wound Care* 1992; **1**(4): 44–53
45. Tatnall FM, Leigh IM, Gibson JR. Comparative study of antiseptic toxicity on basal keratinocytes, transformed human keratinocytes and fibroblasts. *Skin Pharmacol* 1990; **3**(3): 157–163
46. Cannavo M, Fairbrother G, Owen D, Ingle J, Lumley T. *J Wound Care* 1998; **7**(2): 57–62
47. Burgess B. An investigation of hydrocolloids. A comparative prospective randomised trial of the performance of three hydrocolloid dressings. *Professional Nurse* Supplement 1993; **8**(7): 3–6
48. Glyantsev SP, Adamyan AA, Sakharov IYu. Crab collagenase in wound debridement. *J Wound Care* 1997; **6**(1): 13–16
49. Thomas S, Fear M. Comparing two dressings for wound debridement. *J Wound Care* 1993; **2**(5): 272–274
50. Colin D, Kurring PA, Quinlan D, Yvon C. Managing sloughy pressure sores. *J Wound Care* 1996; **5**(10): 444–446
51. Thomas S, Fisher B, Fram PJ, Waring MJ. Odour-absorbing dressings. *J Wound Care* 1998; **7**(5): 246–250
52. Bowler PG, Davies BJ, Jones SA. Microbial involvement in chronic wound malodour. *J Wound Care* 1999; **8:** 216–218
53. Morgan DA. *Wound Cleansing Agents*. Educational Leaflet No. 10 (Parts 1 and 2). The Wound Care Society 1992
54. Bradley M, Cullum N, Sheldon T. The debridement of chronic wounds: a systematic review. *Health Technol Assess* 1999; **3** (17 Pt 1)
55. Bowler *et al.* The viral barrier properties of some occlusive dressings and their control in infection control. *Wounds* 1993; **5**(1): 1–8
56. EL (88) CO/10 (Sept. 5)
57. Baker J. Essential oils: a complementary therapy in wound management. *J Wound Care* 1998; **7**(7): 355–357
58. Leaper DJ. Eusol (Editorial). *Br Med J* 1992; **304:** 930–931

59. Payne CMER *et al.* Argyria from excessive use of topical silver sulphadiazine. *Lancet* 1992; **340:** 126 (letter)
60. Bugmann Ph, Taylor S, Gyger D et al. A silicone-coated nylon dressing reduces healing time in burned paediatric patients in comparison with standard sulfadiazine treatment: a prospective randomised trial. *Burns* 1998; 24: 609–612
61. Thomas S, Loveless P. Examining the properties and uses of two hydrogel sheet dressings. *J Wound Care* 1993; **2**(3): 176–179
62. Thomas S, Banks V, Bale S, Fear-Price M, Hagelstein S, Harding KG, Orpin J, Thomas N. A comparison of two dressings in the management of chronic wounds. *J Wound Care* 1997; **6**(8): 383–386
63. Young SR, Dyson M, Hickman R, Lang S, Osborn C. Comparison of the effects of semi-occlusive polyurethane dressings and hydrocolloid dressings on dermal repair: 1. Cellular changes. *J Invest Dermatol* 1991; **97**: 586–592
64. Phillips TJ, Palko MJ, Bhawan J. Histologic evaluation of chronic human wounds treated with hydrocolloid and non-hydrocolloid dressings. *J Am Acad Dermatol* 1994; **30:** 61–64
65. Glover M. Growth Factors and Wound Healing. *Wound Management* 1992; **2**(1): 9–11
66. Hopkinson I. Growth Factors and extracellular matrix biosynthesis. *J Wound Care* 1992; **1**(2): 47–50
67. Falanga V. Growth Factors and Wound Repair. *J Tissue Viability* 1992; **2**(3): 101–104
68. Arnold F, O'Brien J, Cherry G. Granulocyte monocyte-colony stimulating factor as an agent for wound healing. *J Wound Care* 1995; **4**(9): 400–402
69. Singer AJ, Clark RAF. Cutaneous wound healing. *New Engl J Med* 1999; **341**(10): 738–746
70. Garrett B, Garrett SB. Cellular communication and the action of growth factors during wound healing. *J Wound Care* 1997; **6**(6): 277–280
71. Zumla A, Lulet A. Honey—a remedy rediscovered. *J Roy Soc Med* 1989; **82:** 384–385
72. Willix DJ, Molan PC, Harfoot CG. A comparison of the sensitivity of wound-infecting species of bacteria to the antibacterial activity of manuka honey and other honey. *J Appl Bact* 1992; **73:** 388–394
73. Molan PC. A brief review of honey as a clinical dressing. *Primary Intention* 1998; **6**(4): 148–158
74. Molan PC. The role of honey in the management of wounds. *J Wound Care* 1999; **8**(8): 415–418
75. Subrahmanyam M. A prospective clinical and histological study of superficial burn wound healing with honey and silver sulfadiazine. *Burns* 1998; **24**(2): 157–161
76. Cooper R, Molan PC. The use of honey as an antiseptic in managing Pseudomonas infection. *J Wound Care* 1999; **8**(4): 161–164
77. Cooper RA, Molan PC. Honey in wound care. *J Wound Care* 1999; **8**(7): 340
78. Postmes T, Van Den Bogaard AE, Hazen M. Honey for wounds, ulcers and skin graft preservation. *Lancet* 1993; **341:** 756–757 (letter)
79. Rousseau P, Niecestro RM. Comparison of the physicochemical properties of various hydrocolloid dressings. *Wounds* 1991; **3**(1): 43–48
80. Thomas S, Loveless P. A comparative study of the properties of six hydrocolloid dressings. *Pharm J* 1991; **247:** 672–675
81. Hutchinson JJ. A prospective clinical trial of wound dressings to investigate the rate of infection under occlusion. In: Proceedings of the 3rd European Conference on Advances in Wound Management, eds, Harding KG, Dealey C, Cherry & Finn Gottrup, 1994; 93–96. London: Macmillan Magazines
82. Hutchinson JJ, Lawrence JC. Wound infection under occlusive dressings. *J Hosp Infect* 1991; **17:** 83–94
83. Gill D. The use of hydrocolloids in the treatment of diabetic foot. *J Wound Care* 1999; **8**(4): 204–206
84. Agren M. The cytocompatibility of hydrocolloid dressings. *J Wound Care* 1997; **6**(6): 272–274
85. Sleigh JW, Linter SPK. Hazards of hydrogen peroxide. *Br Med J* 1985; **291:** 1706
86. *Journal of the Medical Defence Union* (Winter, 1988)

87. Simon RH, Scoggin CH, Patterson D. Hydrogen peroxide causes the fatal injury to human fibroblasts exposed to oxygen radicals. *J Biological Chemistry* 1981; **256:** 7181–7186

88. Schmidt RJ, Chung LY, Andrews AM, Turner TD. Hydrogen peroxide is a murine (L929) fibroblast cell proliferant at micro- to manomolar concentrations. In: Proceedings of 1st European Conference on Advances in Wound Management, eds Harding KG, Leaper DL, Turner TD 1992: 117–120. London: Macmillan

89. McKenna PJ, Lehr GS, Leist P, Welling RE. Antiseptic effectiveness with fibroblast preservation. *Annals of Plastic Surgery* 1991; **27:** 265–268

90. Greenway SE. Filler LE. Greenway FL. Topical insulin in wound healing: a randomised, double-blind, placebo-controlled trial. *J Wound Care* 1999; **8**(10): 526–528

91. Bale S, Banks V, Harding KG. A comparison of two amorphous hydrogels in the debridement of pressure sores. *J Wound Care* 1998; **7**(2): 65–68

92. Thomas S. Assessing the hydro-affinity of hydrogel dressings. *J Wound Care* 1994; **3**(2): 89–91

93. Gilchrist B. Should iodine be reconsidered in wound management. *J Wound Care* 1997; **6** (3): 148–150

94. Kero M *et al.* A comparison of Cadexomer Iodine with Dextranomer in the treatment of venous leg ulcers. *Curr Therap Res* 1987 (Nov); **42**(5): 761–767

95. Martin SJ, Corrado OJ, Kay EA. Enzymatic debridement for necrotic wounds. *J Wound Care* 1996; **5**(7): 310–311

96. Thomas S, Andrews A, Hay P, Bourgoise S. The anti-microbial activity of maggot secretions: results of a preliminary study. *J Tissue Viability* 1999; **9**(6): 127–132)

97. Thomas S, Jones M. Maggots and the battle against MRSA: an ancient solution to a modern problem. Biosurgical Research Unit, Bridgend 2000

98. Thomas S, Andrews A, Jones M. The use of larval therapy in wound management. *J Wound Care* 1998; **7**(10): 521–524

99. Courtenay M. The use of larval therapy in wound management in the UK. *J Wound Care* 1999; **8**(4): 177–179

100. Wayman J, Nirojogi V, Walker A, Sowinski A, Walker MA. The cost effectiveness of larval therapy in venous ulcers. *J Tissue Viability* 2000; **10**(3): 91–94

101. Banks V, Bale S, Harding KG. A comparative study to evaluate the effectiveness of Lyofoam A in the treatment of superficial pressure sores. In: Proceedings of the 3rd European Conference on Advances in Wound Management, eds, Harding KG, Dealey C, Cherry & Finn Gottrup; 1994; 21–24. London: Macmillan Magazines

102. Morgan DA. Myiasis: The rise and fall of maggot therapy. *J Tissue Viability* 1995; **5**(2): 43–51

103. Thomas S, Jones M, Shutler S, Jones S. Using larvae in modern wound management. *J Wound Care* 1996; **5**(2): 60–69

104. Thomas S, Andrews A. The effect of hydrogel dressings on maggot development. *J Wound Care* 1999; **8**(2): 75–77)

105. Bugmann Ph, Taylor S, Gyger D *et al.* A silicone-coated nylon dressing reduces healing time in burned paediatric patients in comparison with standard sulfadiazine treatment: a prospective randomised trial. *Burns* 1998; **24:** 609–612

106. Editorial. Management of Smelly Tumours. *Lancet* 1990; **355:** 141–142

107. Thompson Rice J. Metronidazole use in malodorous skin lesions. *Rehabilitation Nursing* 1992; **17**(5): 244–245, 255

108. *Drug Therap Bull* 1992; **30**(18): 18–19

109. Hampson JP. The use of metronidazole in the treatment of malodorous wounds. *J Wound Care* 1996; **5**(9): 421–426

110. Lawrence JC, Kidson A, Lilly HA. An adherent semi-permeable film dressing for burns. *J Wound Care* 1992; **1**(2): 10–11

111. *Drug Therap Bull* 1992; 20th Jan: 7–8

112. *Arch Derm* 1984; **120:** 640–645

113. Greif R, Akca O, Horn E-P, Kurz A, Sessler DI. Supplemental perioperative oxygen to reduce the incidence of surgical-wound infection. *N Engl J Med* 2000; **342:** 161–167
114. Powell SM *et al.* Patch test study of a new medicated paste bandage in patients with chronic leg ulcers. In: Proceedings of the 4th European Conference on Advances in Wound Management, eds, Cherry GW, Leaper DJ, Lawrence JC, Milward P. 1995; 66–68. London, Macmillan Magazines
115. Stacey MC, Jopp-Mckay AG, Rashid P, Hoskin SE, Thompson PJ. The influence of dressings on venous ulcer healing – a randomised trial. *Eur J Vasc Endovasc Surg* 1997; **13:** 174–179
116. Oxpentifylline for venous leg ulcers. *Drug Therap Bull* 1991; **29:** 59–60
117. Jull AB, Waters J, Arrol B. Oral pentoxifylline for treatment of venous leg ulcers (Cochrane Review). In: *Cochrane Library*, Issue 3, 2000. Oxford: Update Software
118. Dale JJ, Ruckley CV, Harper DR, Gibson B, Nelson EA, Prescott RJ. Randomised, double blind placebo controlled trial of pentoxifylline in the treatment of venous leg ulcers. *Br Med J* 1999; **319:** 875–878
119. Anstead GM, Hart LM, Sunahara JF, Liter ME. Phenytoin in wound healing. *Ann Pharmacother* 1996; **30:** 768–775
120. Lodha SC *et al.* Role of phenytoin in healing of large abscess cavities. *Br J Surg* 1991; **78:** 105–108
121. Gilmore OJA, Reid C, Strokon A. A study of the effect of povidone-iodine on wound healing. *Postgrad Med J* 1977; **53:** 617, 122–125
122. Waran KD, Munsick RA. Anaphylaxis from povidone-iodine. *Lancet* 1995; **345:** 1506
123. Thomas C. Nursing Alert—Wound Healing halted with the use of povidone-iodine. *Ostomy/Wound Management* 1988; **18**(Spring): 30–33
124. Rodeheaver G. Controversies in topical wound management. *Ostomy/Wound Management* 1988; **18**(Fall): 58–68
125. Goldenheim PD. An appraisal of povidone-iodine and wound healing. (Review). *Postgrad Med J* 1993; **69**(suppl 3): S97–S105
126. Welch JS. (Letter to Editor). *Ostomy/Wound Management* 1991; **35:** 28–29
127. Fenton AH, Warren M. Release of medicament from proflavine cream. *Pharm J* 1962; **188:** 5
128. Gupta R, Foster ME, Miller E. Calcium alginate in the management of acute surgical wounds and abscesses. *J Tissue Viability* 1991; **1**(4): 115–116
129. Sawada Y, Sone K. Treatment of scars and keloids with a cream containing silicone oil. *Br J Plast Surg* 1990; **43:** 683–688
130. Sawada Y, Sone K. Beneficial effects of silicone cream on grafted skin. *Br J Plast Surg* 1992; **45:** 105–108
131. Jones JE, Nelson EA. Skin grafting for venous leg ulcers (Cochrane Review). In: *The Cochrane Library*, Issue 3, 2000. Oxford: Update Software
132. Dealey C. Using protective skin wipes under adhesive tapes. *J Wound Care* 1992; **1**(2): 19–22
133. Mulder GT. The role of tissue engineering in wound care. *J Wound Care* 1999; **8**(1): 21–24.
134. *Pharm J* 2000; **264:** 87
135. Banks V, Harding KG. Comparing two dressings for exuding pressure sores in community patients. *J Wound Care* 1994; **3**(4): 175–178
136. Banks V, Bale S, Harding KG. The use of two dressings for moderately exuding pressure sores. *J Wound Care* 1994; **3**(3): 132–134
137. Tsakayannis D *et al.* Sucralfate and chronic venous stasis ulcers. *Lancet* 1994; **343:** 424–425
138. Topham J. Sugar for wounds. *J Tissue Viability* 2000; **10**(3): 86–89
139. Middleton KR, Seal D. Sugar as an aid to wound healing. *Pharm J* 1985; **235:** 757–758
140. Archer *et al.* A controlled model of moist wound healing: comparison between semi-permeable film, antiseptics and sugar paste. *J Exp Path* 1990; **71:** 155–170
141. *Antimicrob Agents Chemother* 1991; **35**(9): 1799–1803
142. Anon. Cleansing wounds with tap water. *J Wound Care* 1994; **3**(2): 65
143. Angeras AD *et al.* Comparison between sterile saline and tap water for the cleansing of acute traumatic soft tissue wounds. *Eur J Surg* 1992; **158**(33): 347–350
144. Riyat MS, Quinton DN. Tap water as a wound cleansing agent in accident and emergency. *J Acc Emerg Med* 1997; **14:** 165–166

145. Lawrence JC. Medicated tulle dressings. *J Wound Care* 1993; **2**(4): 240–243
146. Baxandall T. Healing cavity wounds with negative pressure. *Nursing Standard* 1996; **11**(6): 49–51
147. Thomas S. Vapour-permeable film dressings. *J Wound Care* 1996; **5**(6): 271–274
148. Thomas S, Loveless P, Hay NP. Comparative review of the properties of six semi-permeable film dressings. *Pharm J* 1988; **240**: 785–789
149. Hoffmann *et al.* Transparent polyurethane film as an intravenous catheter dressing. A meta-analysis of the infection risks. *JAMA* 1992; **267**(15): 2072–2076
150. McKeeman K, Wallace P. Bring Varidase use into line. A drug use evaluation of Varidase Topical solution. *Pharmacy in Practice* 1995; September: 336–339
151. Green C. Antistreptokinase titres after topical streptokinase. *Lancet* 1993; **341**: 1602–1603
152. Bux M, Baig MK, Rodrigues E, Armstrong D, Brown A. Antibody response to topical streptokinase *J Wound Care* 1997; **6**(2): 70–73
153. Wilkinson EAJ, Hawke CI. Does oral zinc aid the healing of chronic leg ulcers? (Cochrane Review). In: *The Cochrane Library*, Issue 4, 1998. Oxford: Update Software
154. Morgan DA. Wound management products in the Drug Tariff. *Pharm J* 1999; **263**: 820–825
155. Morgan DA. Wound Management : Which Dressing? *Pharm J* 1993 ; May **29** : 738–743
156. Guidelines for wound management in Northern Ireland. Clinical Resource Efficiency Support Team. October 1998, Belfast
157. White RJ. The management of exuding wounds. The Wound Care Society. Education Leaflet August 2000;7(3)
158. Berry DP, Jones V. Cavity wound management. *J Wound Care* 1993; **2**(1): 29–32
159. Bale S. Cavity wounds. Educational leaflet No. 11. The Wound Care Society 1993
160. Bale S. A guide to wound debridement. *J Wound Care* 1997; **6**(4): 179–182
161. Tong A. The identification and treatment of slough. *J Wound Care* 1999; **8**: 338–339
162. Vowden KR, Vowden P. Wound debridement, Part 1: non-sharp techniques. *J Wound Care* 1999; **8**: 237–240
163. Dunford C. Hypergranulation tissue. *J Wound Care* 1999; **8**(10): 506–507
164. Harris A, Rolstad BS. Hypergranulation tissue: a non-traumatic method of management. In: Proceedings of the 2nd European Conference on Advances in Wound Management, eds. Harding KG, Cherry G, Dealey C, Turner TD 1993: 35–37
165. The prevention and treatment of pressure sores. *Effective Health Care Bulletin* October 1995, **2**(1).
166. Cullum N, Deeks J, Sheldon TA, Song F, Fletcher AW. Beds, mattresses and cushions for pressure sore prevention and treatment (Cochrane Review). In: *Cochrane Library*, Issue 3, 2000. Oxford: Update Software
167. Wounds: Pressure ulcers. In *Clinical Evidence. A compendium of the best available evidence for effective health care*. BR MED J Publishing Group, issue 2, Dec 1999
168. Complications of diabetes: screening for retinopathy, management of foot ulcers. *Effective Health Care August* 1999; **5**(4). The University of York. NHS Centre for Reviews and Dissemination
169. Spencer S. Pressure relieving interventions for preventing and treating diabetic foot ulcers (Cochrane Review). In: *Cochrane Library*, Issue 3, 2000. Oxford: Update Software
170. Morgan DA. The application of the 'ideal dressing' theory to practice. *Nursing Scotland* 1998; July: 16–18
171. Modern Wound Management Dressings. National Prescribing Centre. *Prescribing Nurse Bulletin* 1999; **1**(2): www.npc.co.uk/
172. Bradley M, Cullum N, Nelson EA, Petticrew M, Torgeson D. Systematic reviews of wound care management: (2) Dressings and topical agents used in the healing of chronic wounds. *Health Technol Assess* 1999; **3** (17 Pt 2)
173. Wounds: Venous leg ulcers. In *Clinical Evidence. A compendium of the best available evidence for effective health care*. BMJ Publishing Group, issue 2, Dec 1999

116

I.D. No. 1355179

**UNIVERSITY OF BRADFORD
LIBRARY**

2 1 AUG 2001

ACCESSION No. 0343504139
CLASS No. WO 196 MOR
LOCATION School of Health
Studies Library